AF328440

William Arnold

Suburban Herbarium

Uniformbooks

First published 2020, reprinted 2022
Copyright © Images: William Arnold
Texts: Mark Cocker, Val Williams
ISBN 978-1-910010-23-5

Uniformbooks
7 Hillhead Terrace, Axminster, Devon EX13 5JL
uniformbooks.co.uk

Trade distribution in the UK by Central Books
centralbooks.com

Printed and bound by T J Books, Padstow, Cornwall

Foreword

At one level *Suburban Herbarium* seems a very simple book. Before you, over the following pages, is a series of one hundred plates of plants, grasses and ferns found on one small geographical plot.

They are black-and-white photographic portraits but, if anything, they seem to convert their vegetable subjects to even deeper levels of simplicity. Instead of the minute details of foliage and flower that one has come to expect from digital macro-photography, here are the organisms represented as minimalist shapes of intense light.

One of my favourites is of hairy bittercress *Cardamine hirsutum*, (page 28) whose evocative name, as well as the plant it describes, is well known to me. I associate the species with deep black peat soils on Norfolk dyke-edges, where the tiny white flowers are washed by weak spring sunlight and blessed by the first bumblebees and orange-tip butterflies. Here is hairy bittercress, however, transformed to a many-fingered fire burning white hot in the night.

Turn now to perhaps the simplest of all of the images, that extraordinary plate on page 16. I know the caption says 'Dutch Garlic *Allium hollandicum*'. To me the vision before you looks like nothing more than a supernova at a point of explosion, a fierce and impossibly bright light spiring into outer space in sixteen separate brilliant trajectories.

Looking at the photograph on page 51 I see that the caption says 'Ash *Fraxinus excelsior*'. I have lived with ash trees as familiars and neighbours all of my life. They are the default species of Derbyshire's limestone dales. That's not an ash stem, surely. It suggests to me the image of a dinosaur's four-toed foot—and look even at the detailed joints in the toes—from one of those little theropod species, whose proto-feathers eventually gave us the entire evolutionary lineage of birds. I could go on: the black-

berry that suggests a firework display, the ox-eye daisy that's
a child's drawing of our sun… but on a stalk.

As I look more generally at the whole collection, I am
reminded of the words of two great philosophers. The first are
from the French poet Paul Valéry, who once wrote "To see is to
forget the name of the thing one sees". What I assume he meant
was that if we look hard and long enough at something then
the physical processes of that genuine seeing will triumph over
any presumed familiarities with an animal or plant. The organ-
ism will cease to be known and ordinary. The tired sheath of
language in which we have trapped the subject will fall away
and it will be revealed afresh in a new and radiant light. That
is exactly what Arnold has achieved. He has made us see the
plants as if for the first time.

From the sublime to the ridiculous, I'm also reminded of
those comic words of Dr Spock. As always, Captain Kirk would
turn to his first lieutenant on the *USS Enterprise* for answers, and
Spock would comb the air around the mysterious object with his
weird whirring box thing, and then announce to his boss: "It's
life, Jim, but not as we know it."

It strikes me that through the alchemy of his photographic
practice Arnold has brought us exactly to this realisation. He
has obliged us to visit a different planet and made us appreciate
how weird and truly wonderful its inhabitants are. Weirdest of
all is the fact that the planet is Earth and we have been here all
along.

To be specific, Arnold's otherworldly place is a section on the
outskirts of Truro in his home county of Cornwall. It happens to
be where he takes his lunch-time walk from his day job at Truro
College. It is also the kind of overlooked, anonymous space that
is such a commonplace feature of English towns and cities, what
the writer Richard Mabey defined as being part of the 'unofficial
countryside'.

They are, in truth, neither rural habitat, nor urban district,
but a hybrid zone where both coexist. For five years William
Arnold has plumbed its unacknowledged depths and found and
documented all the plants, grasses and ferns that have flourished
there in the cracks between the pavements or perhaps along the
edges to the walls.

The artist sees the plant citizens of this no-man's land as overlooked in more senses than one. Not only are they neglected in the manner of the landscape they inhabit, they are also subject to what Arnold calls our 'plant blindness': our unfailing capacity to discount the significance of vegetative life in favour of vertebrate forms like ourselves. Just to give you a single powerful illustration of our plant blindness: the Royal Society for the Protection of Birds has 1.2 million members; its vegetable equivalent called Plantlife UK has 11,000.

This indifference to wild plants is odd, especially in view of our disproportionate obsession with their larger relatives: trees. Just like those arboreal cousins, however, the herbs and lower plants play a central role in regulating all of life on Earth. Half the oxygen you will ever breath is delivered by phytoplankton in the sea that don't even possess a nucleus, let alone a root system and a tree trunk. Arnold makes us think about this. All vegetation matters. We just prefer not to notice.

These haunting plates make us think finally about the artist's own medium and practice. By presenting us with plants that resemble old-style negatives we are reminded of the very origins of photography. We are asked to recall how it was once a new technology that served as an adjunct to the scientific documentation of our physical world. These plates recall that history but they also subvert and comment ironically upon it. Here is a taxonomy in the grand manner of the nineteenth century, but recording a modern non-place and its overlooked plant inhabitants.

Mark Cocker contributes regularly to the *Guardian*, the *Times Literary Supplement*, as well as BBC Radio Four. His book *Crow Country* was shortlisted for the Samuel Johnson Prize 2008 and won the New Angle Prize for Literature 2009. With the photographer David Tipling he published *Birds and People* in 2013; *Our Place: Can We Save Britians Wildlife Before It Is Too Late?* was shortlisted for the Wainwright Golden Beer Book Prize 2019; his most recent book *A Claxton Diary: Further Field Notes from a Small Planet*, was overall Book of the Year in the East Anglian Book Awards 2019.

Suburban Herbarium

"I was indeed a stranger in a strange land, yet I was still under the protecting eye of that God who has condescended to call himself the stranger's friend. At this moment, painful as my reflections were, the extraordinary beauty of a small moss in fructification irresistibly caught my eye. I mention this to show from what trifling circumstances the mind will sometimes draw consolation; for though the whole plant was not larger than the top of one of my fingers, I could not contemplate the delicate conformation of its roots, leaves, and capsula, without admiration."

—Mungo Park, *Travels in the Interior Districts of Africa*, 1799

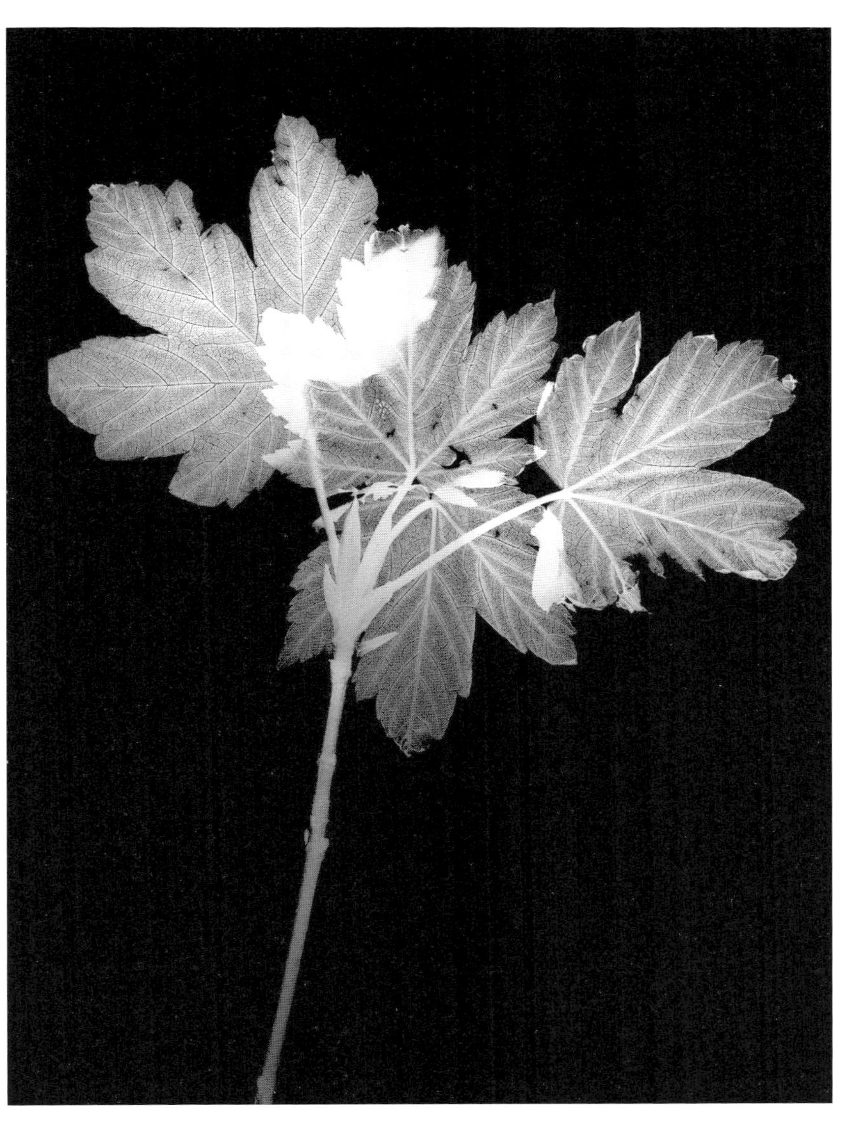

Sycamore
Acer pseudoplatanus

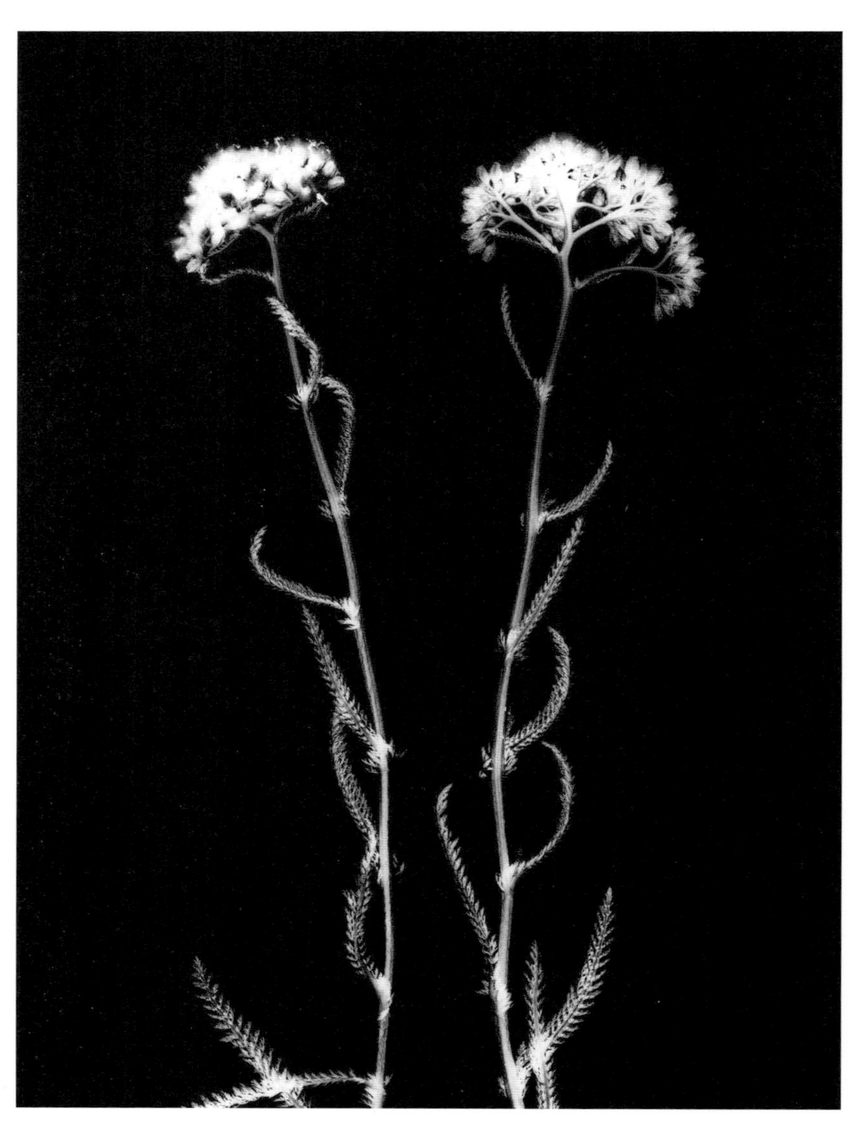

Yarrow

Achillea millefolium

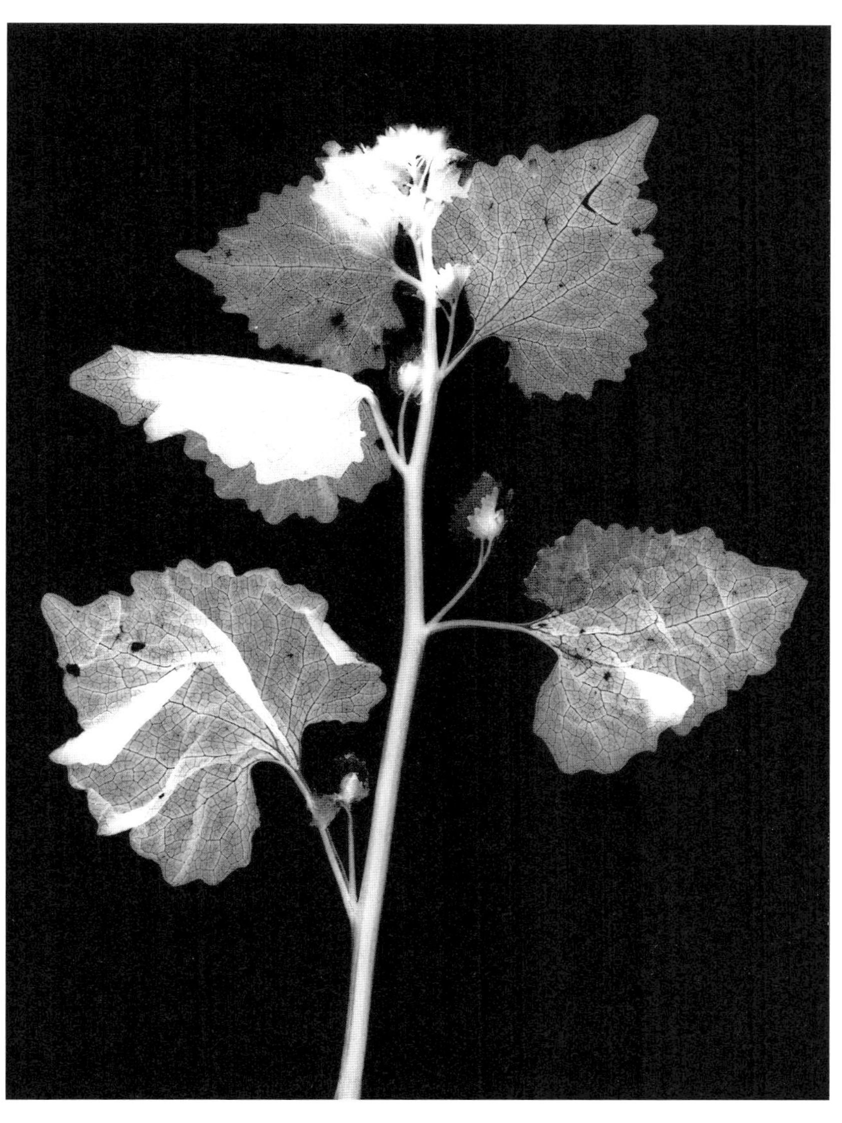

Jack-by-the-hedge
Alliaria petiolata

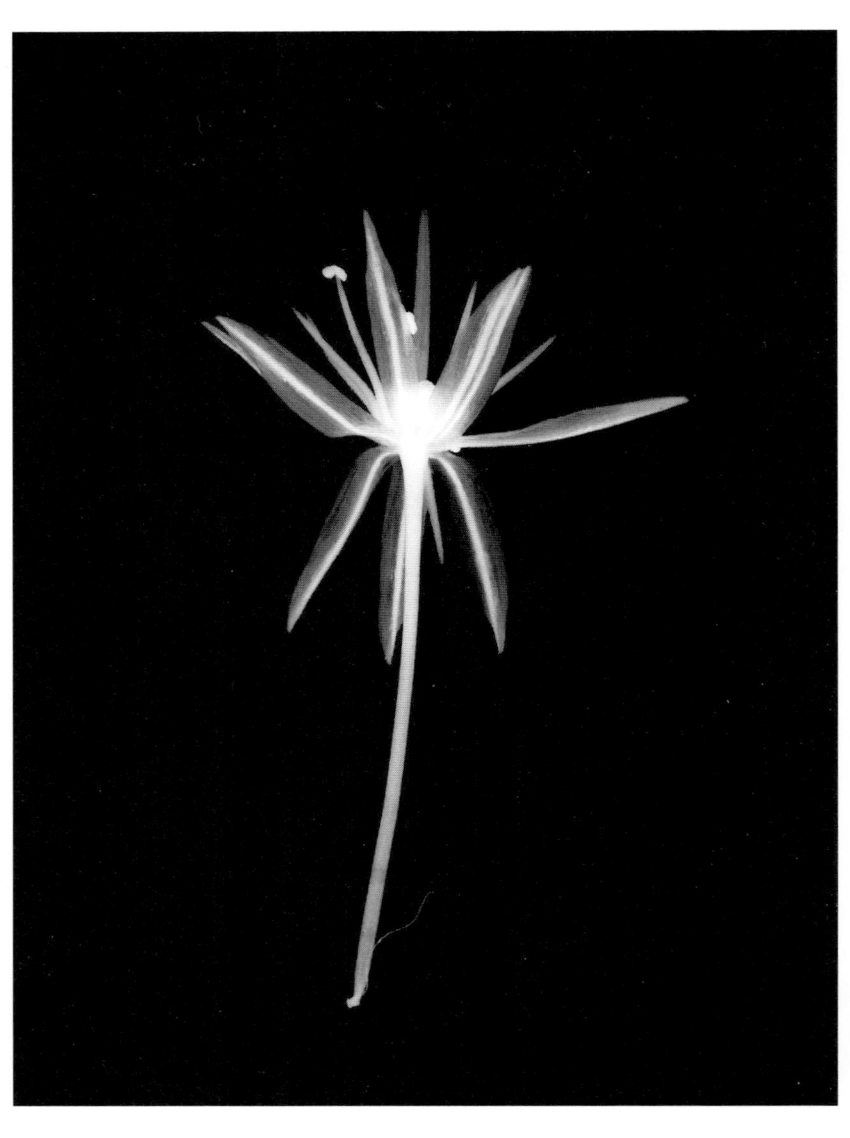

Dutch Garlic (single flower)
Allium hollandicum

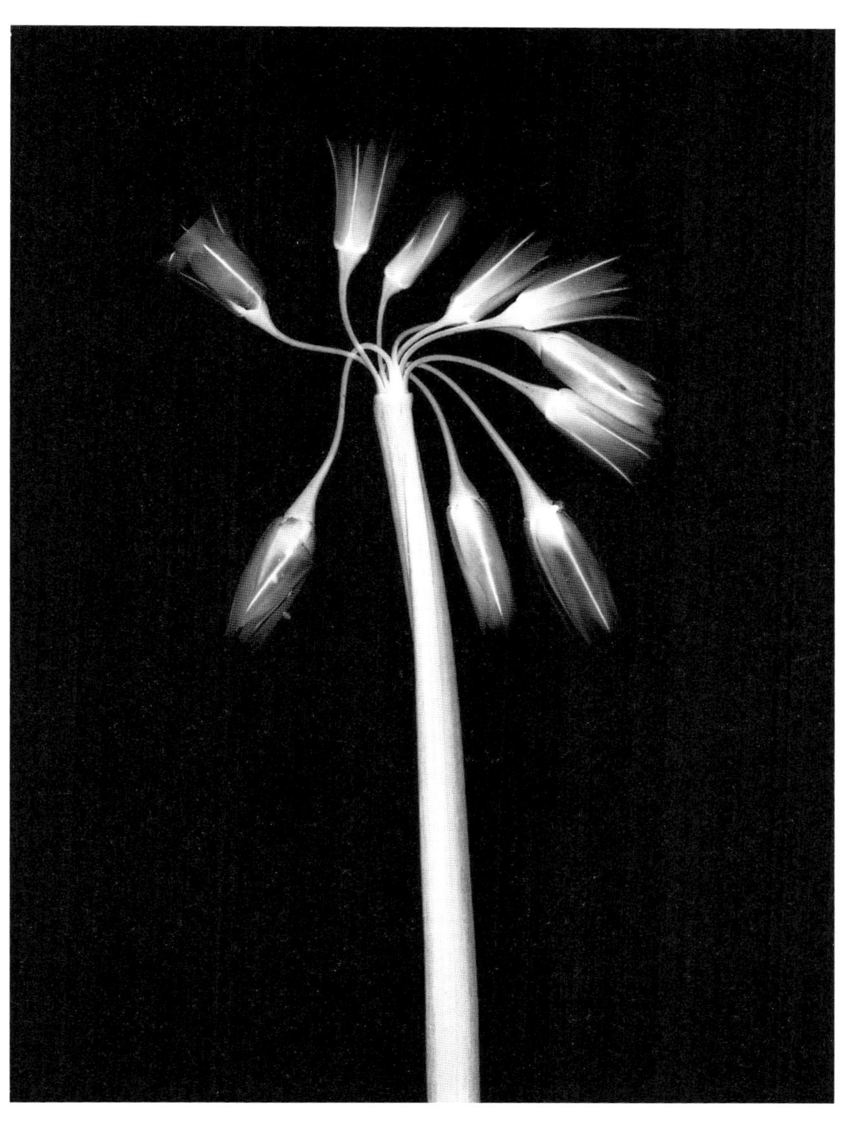

Three-cornered Leek
Allium triquetrum

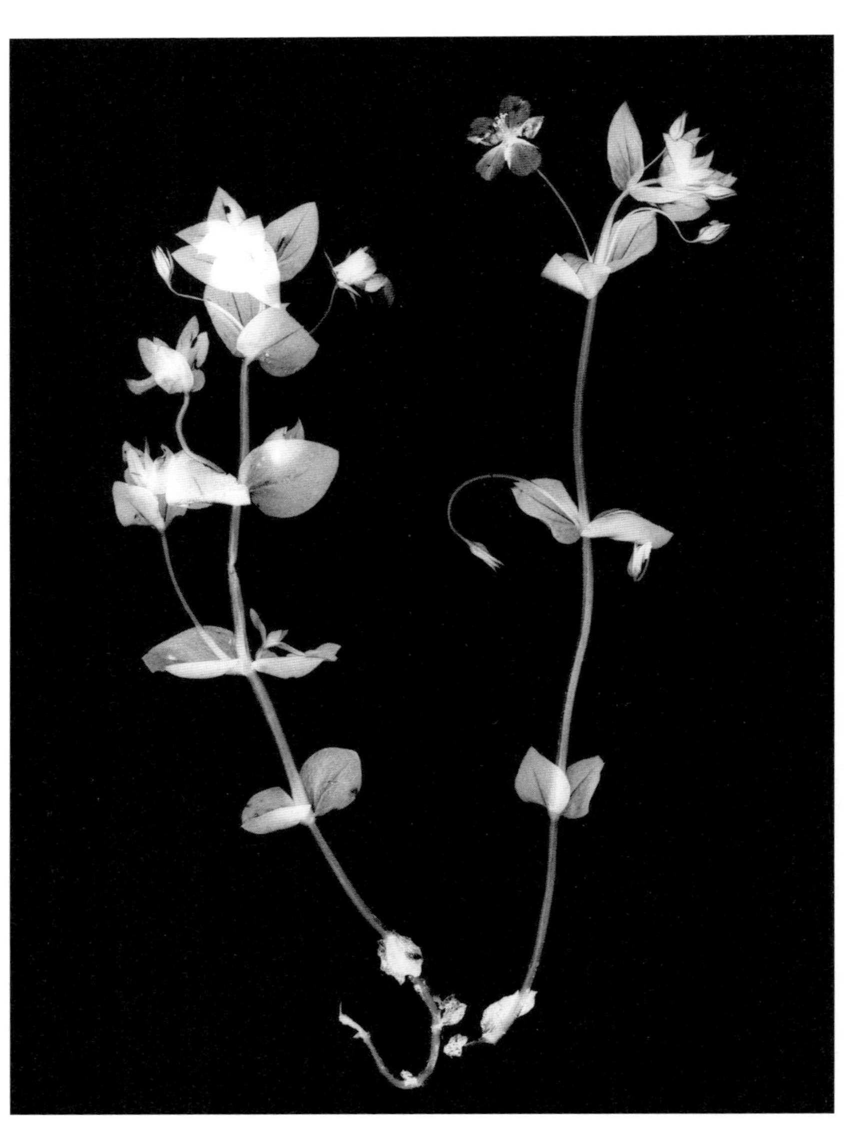

Scarlet Pimpernel
Anagallis arvensis

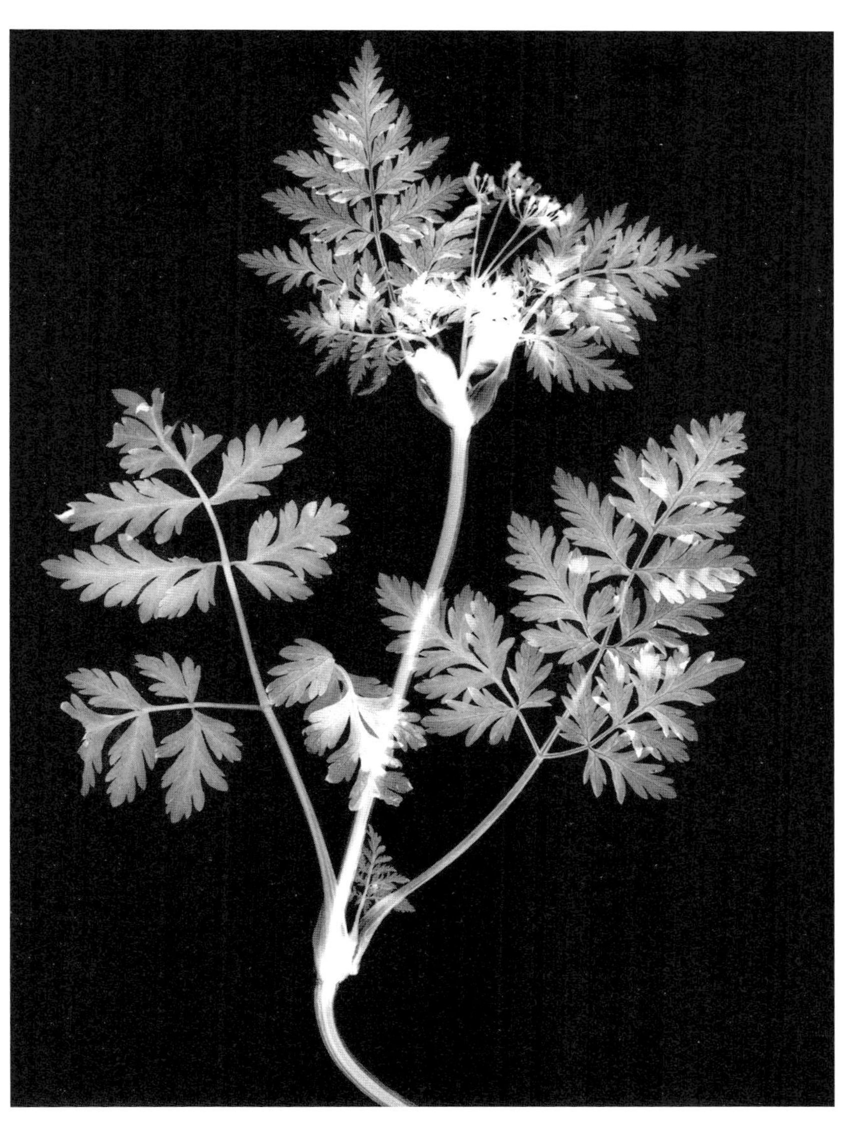

Cow Parsley
Anthriscus sylvestris

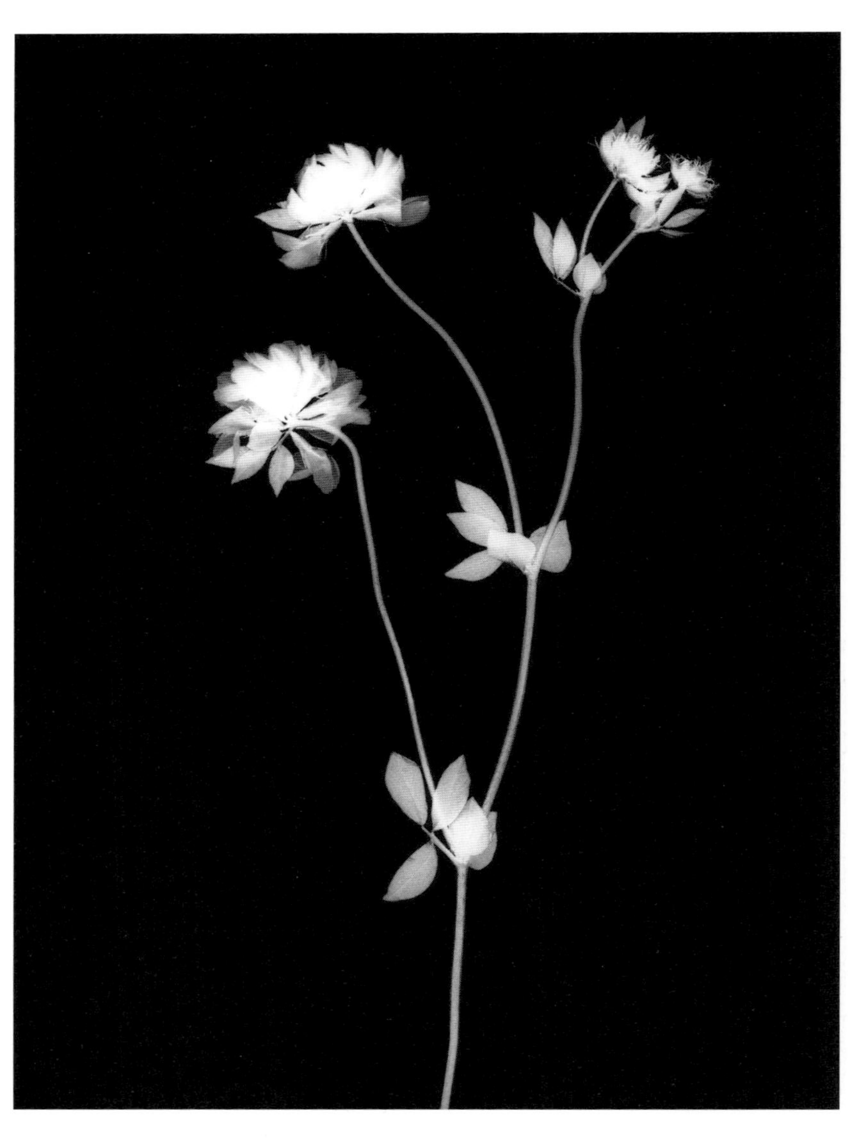

Kidney Vetch
Anthyllis vulneraria

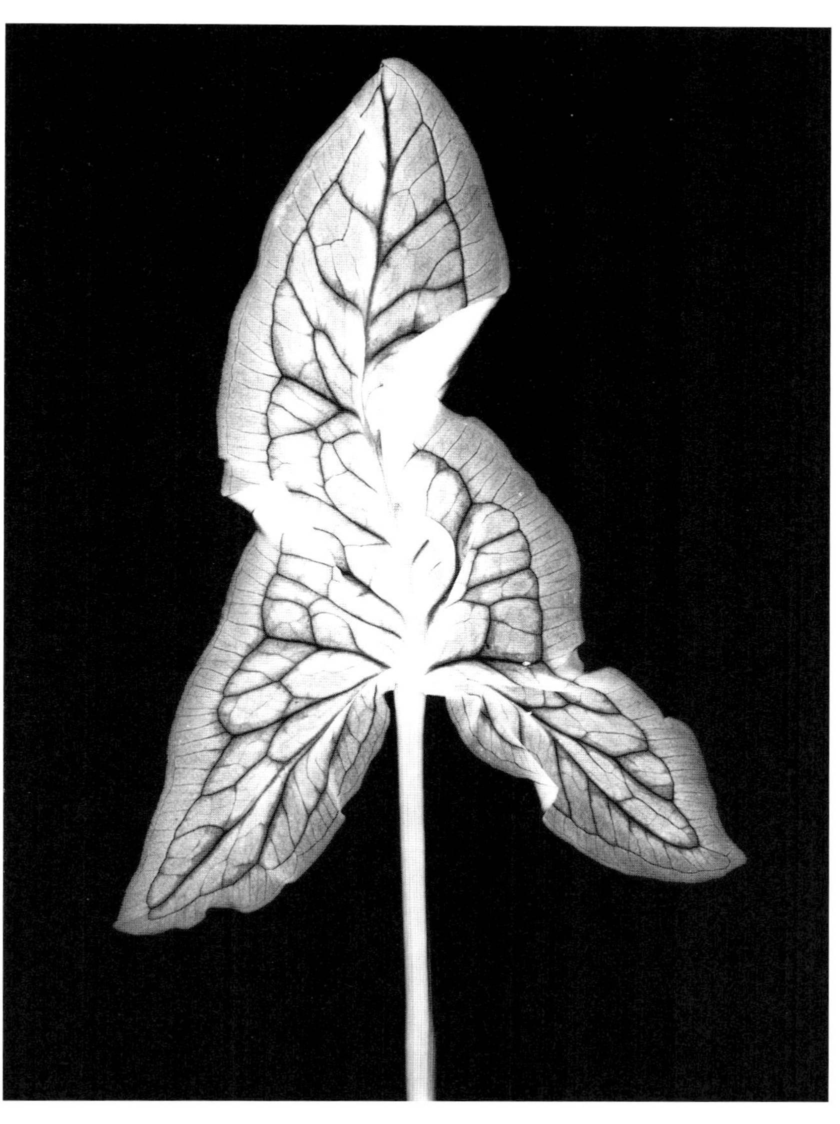

Lords-and-ladies
Arum maculatum

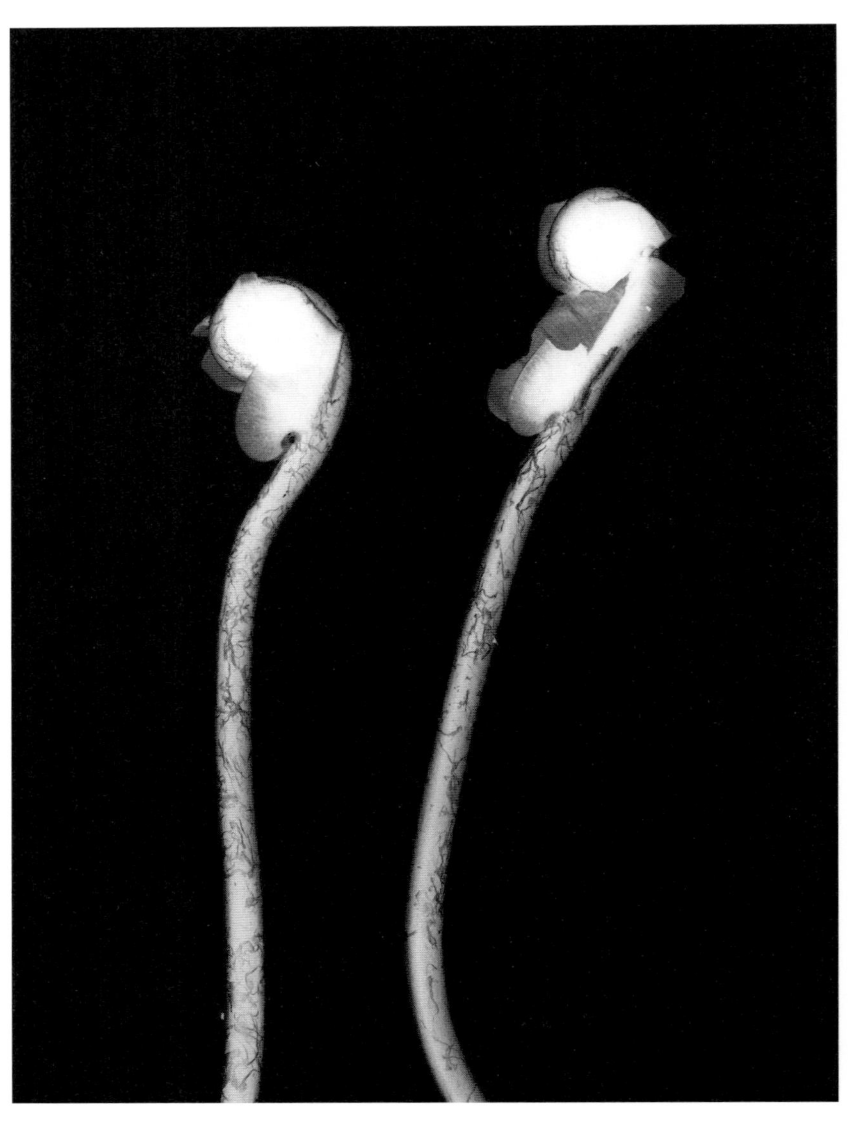

Hart's-tongue Fern
Asplenium scolopendrium

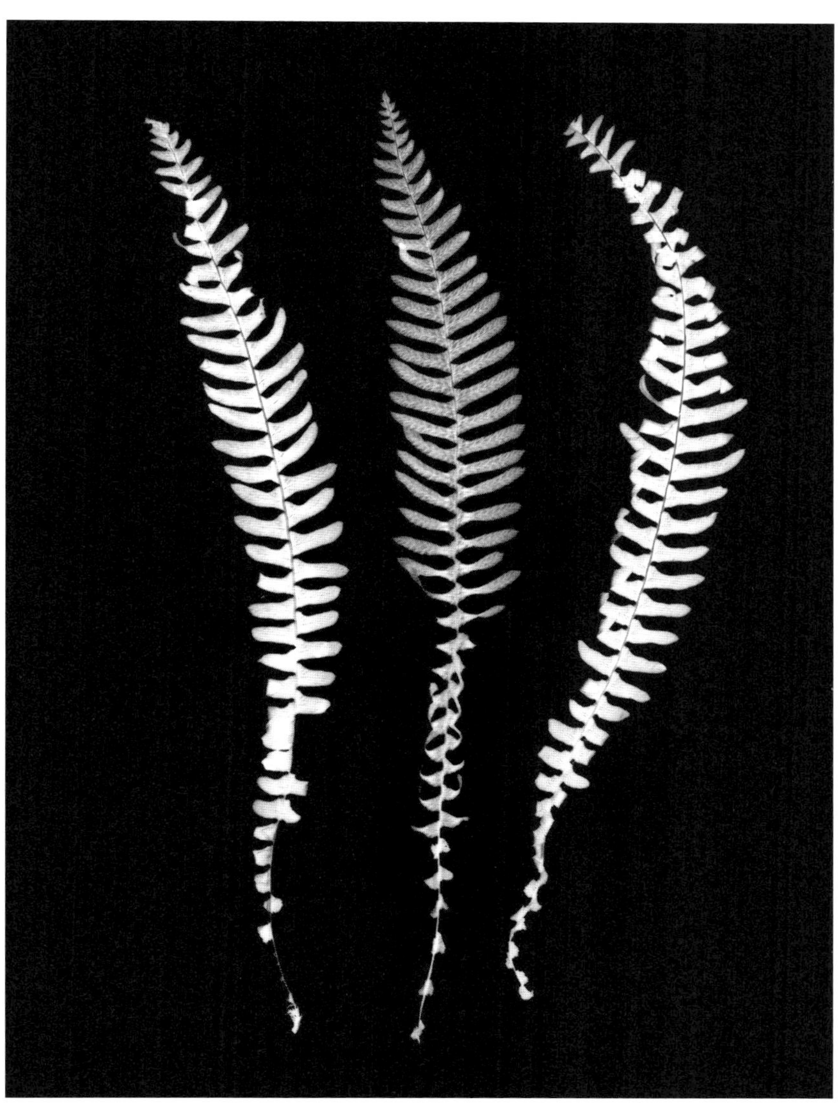

Hard Fern
Blechnum spicant

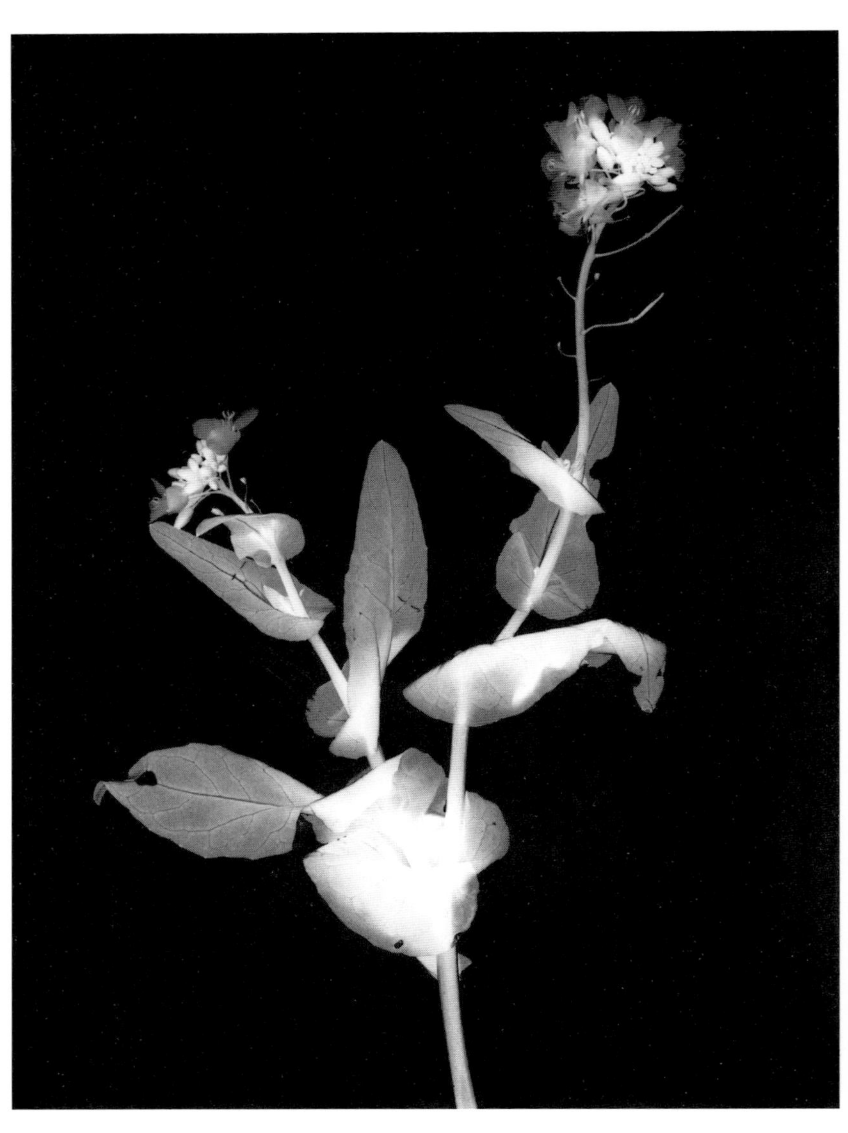

Wild Turnip
Brassica rapa

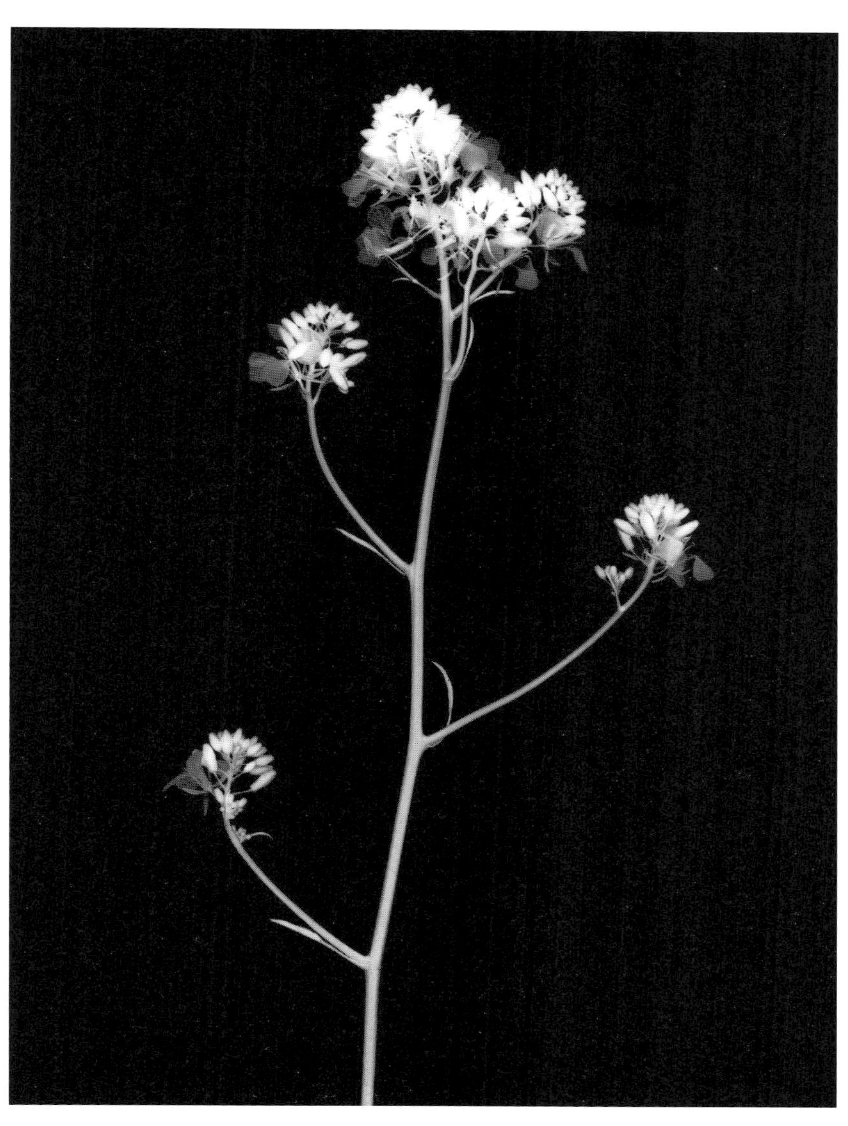

Rapeseed
Brassica napus

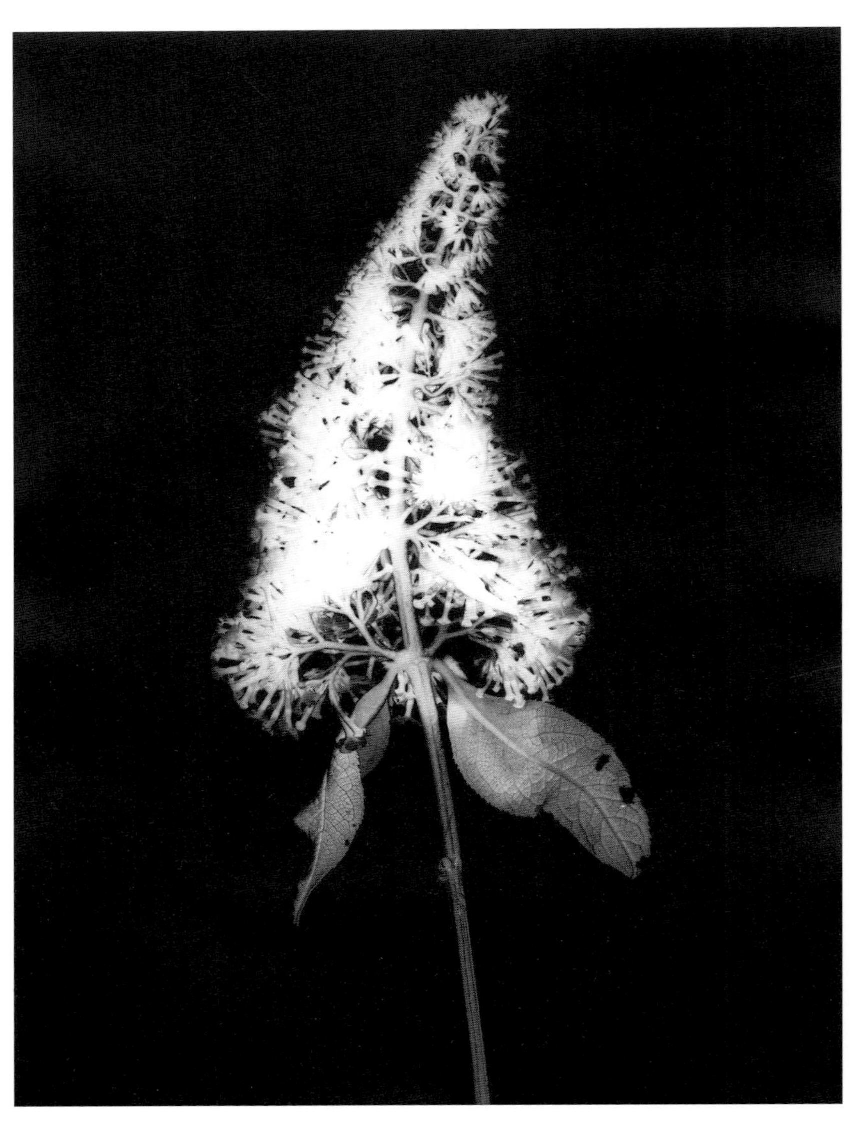

Buddleia
Buddleia davidii

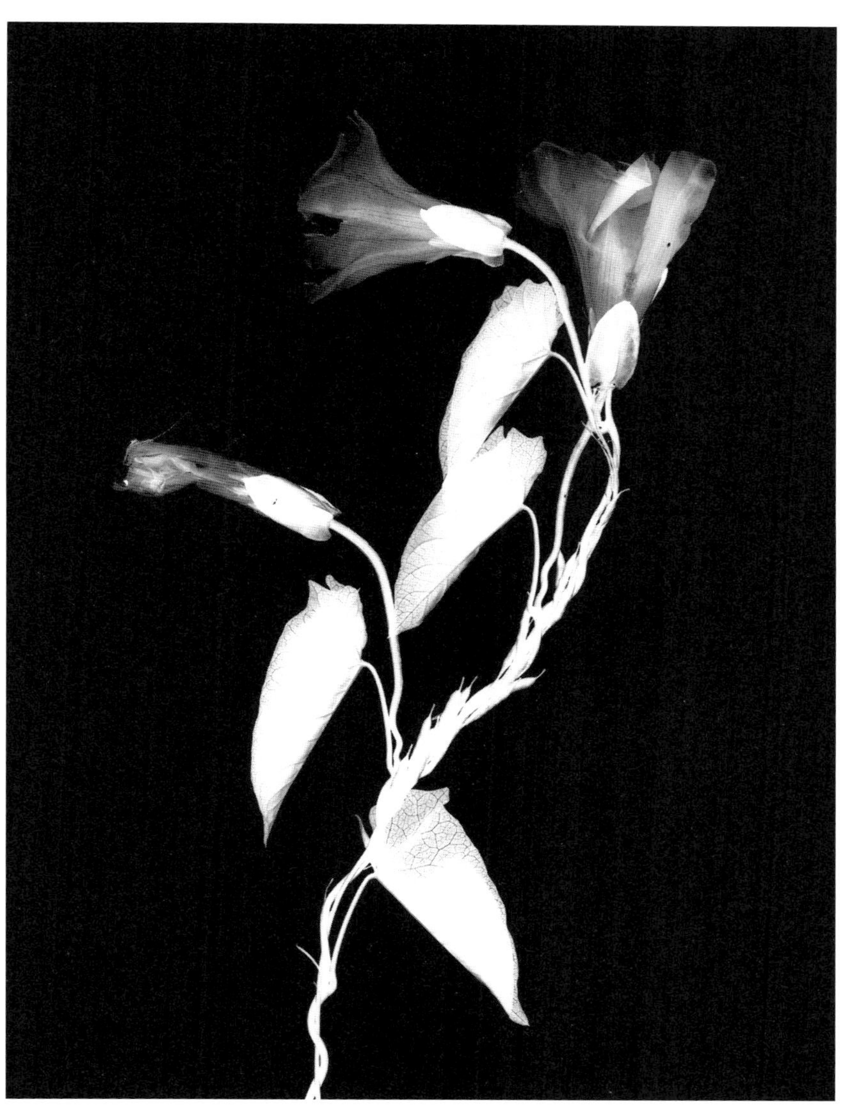

Hedge Bindweed
Calystegia sepium

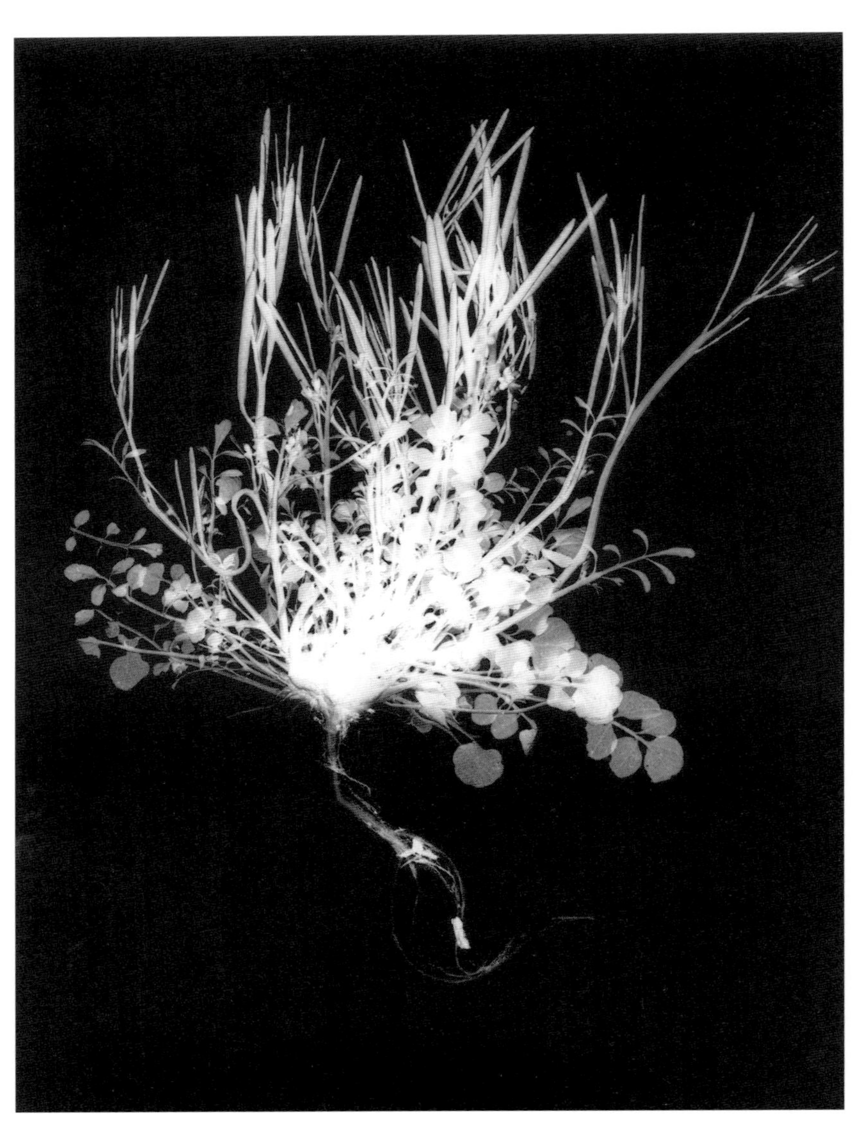

Hairy Bittercress
Cardamine hirsutum

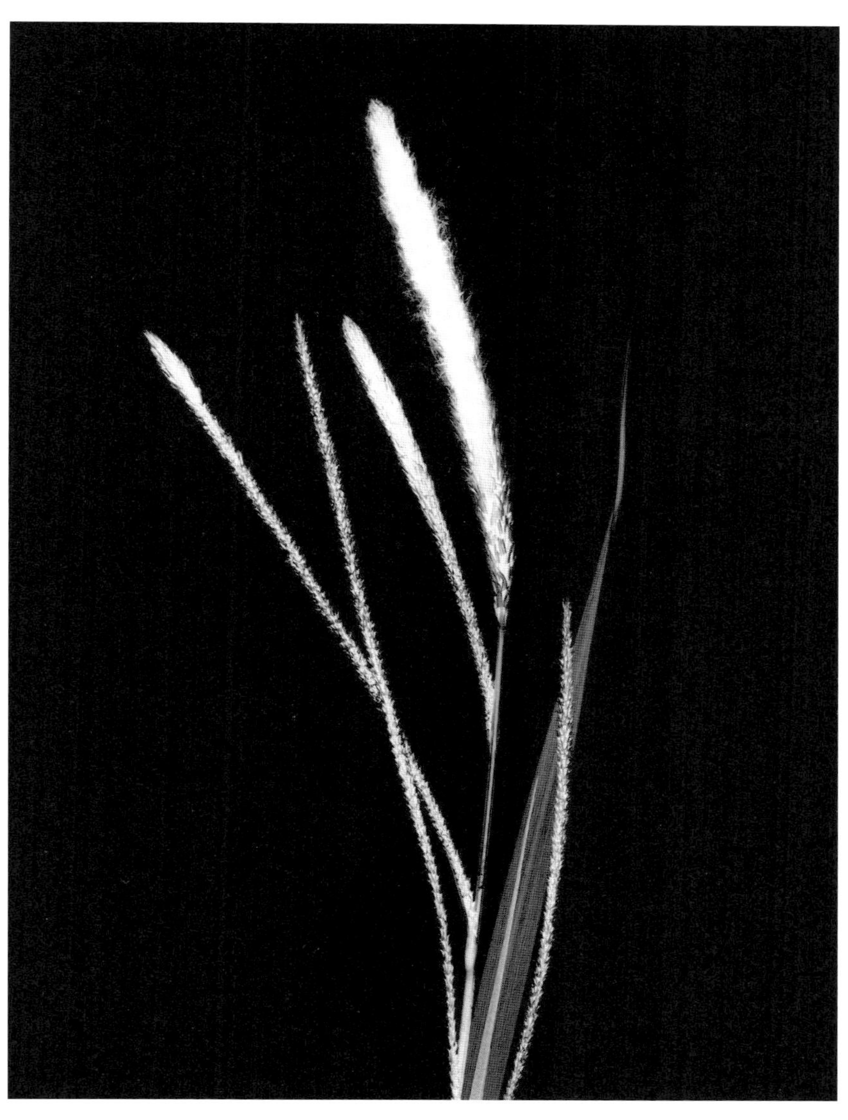

Pendulous Sedge
Carex pendula

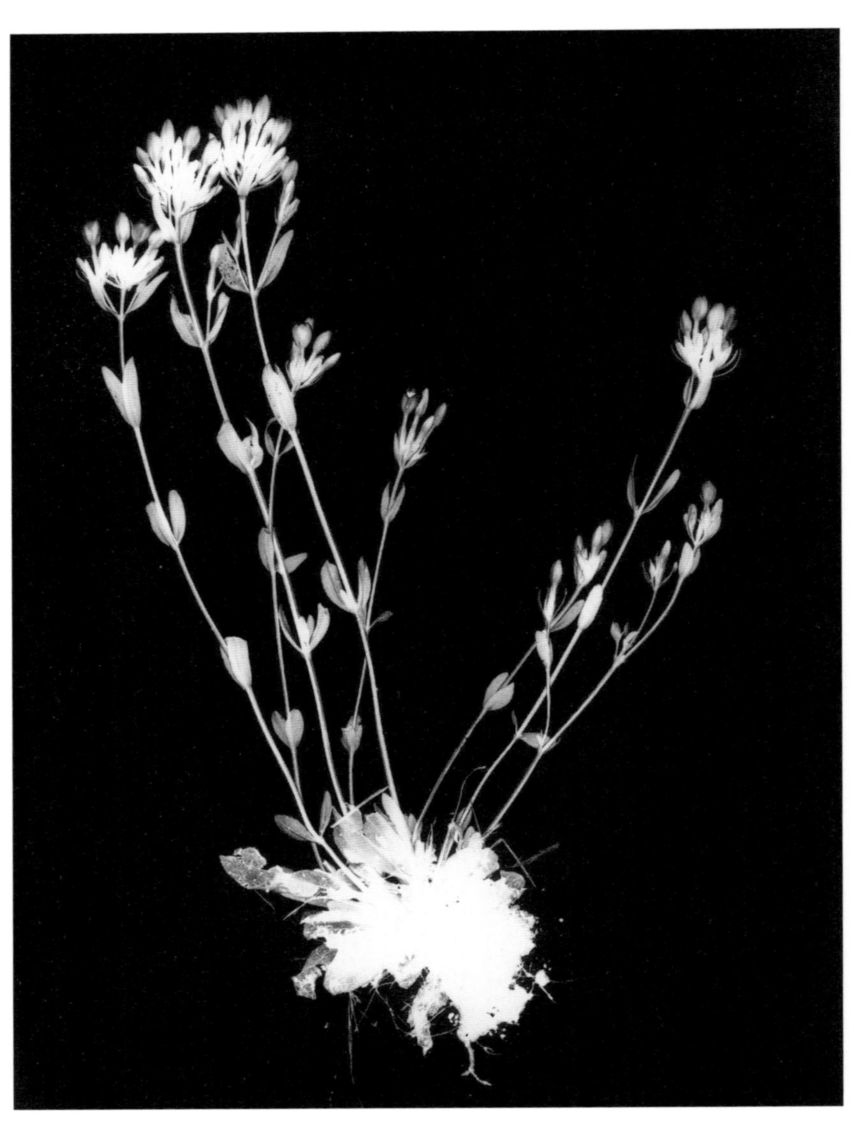

Common Centaury
Centaurium erythraea

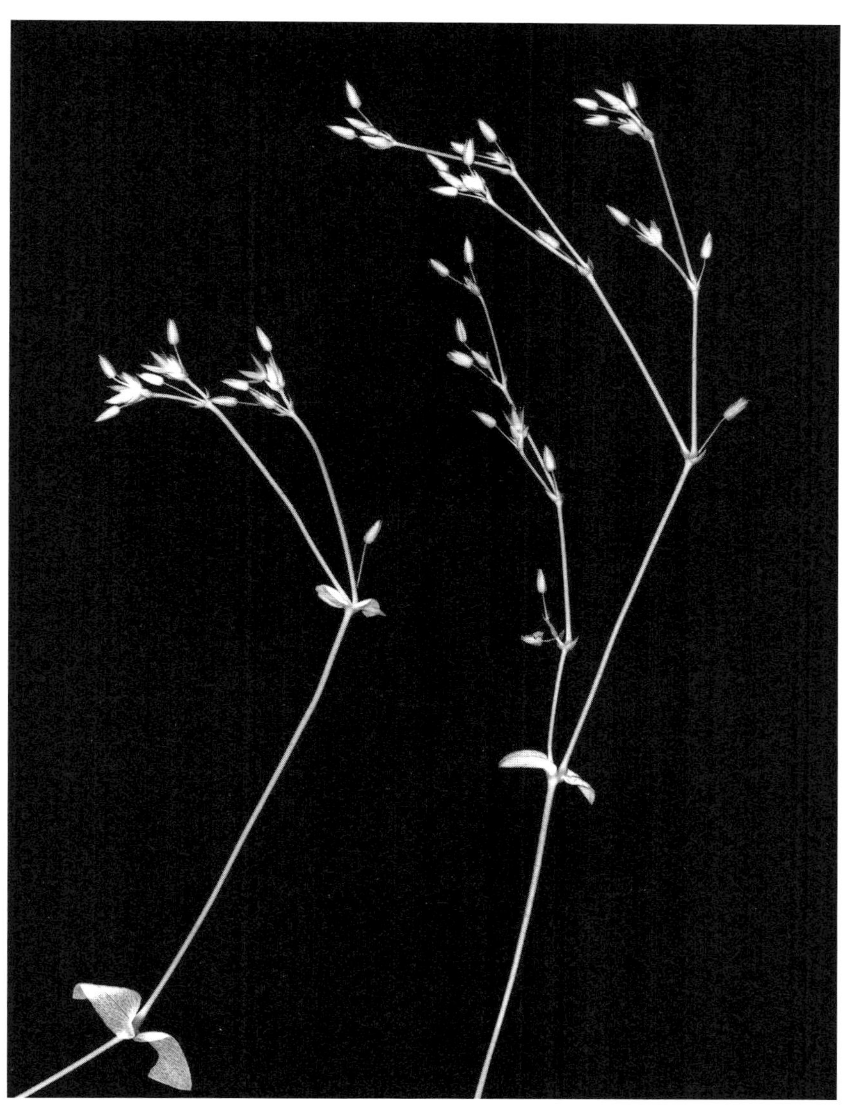

Common Mouse-ear
Cerastium fontanum

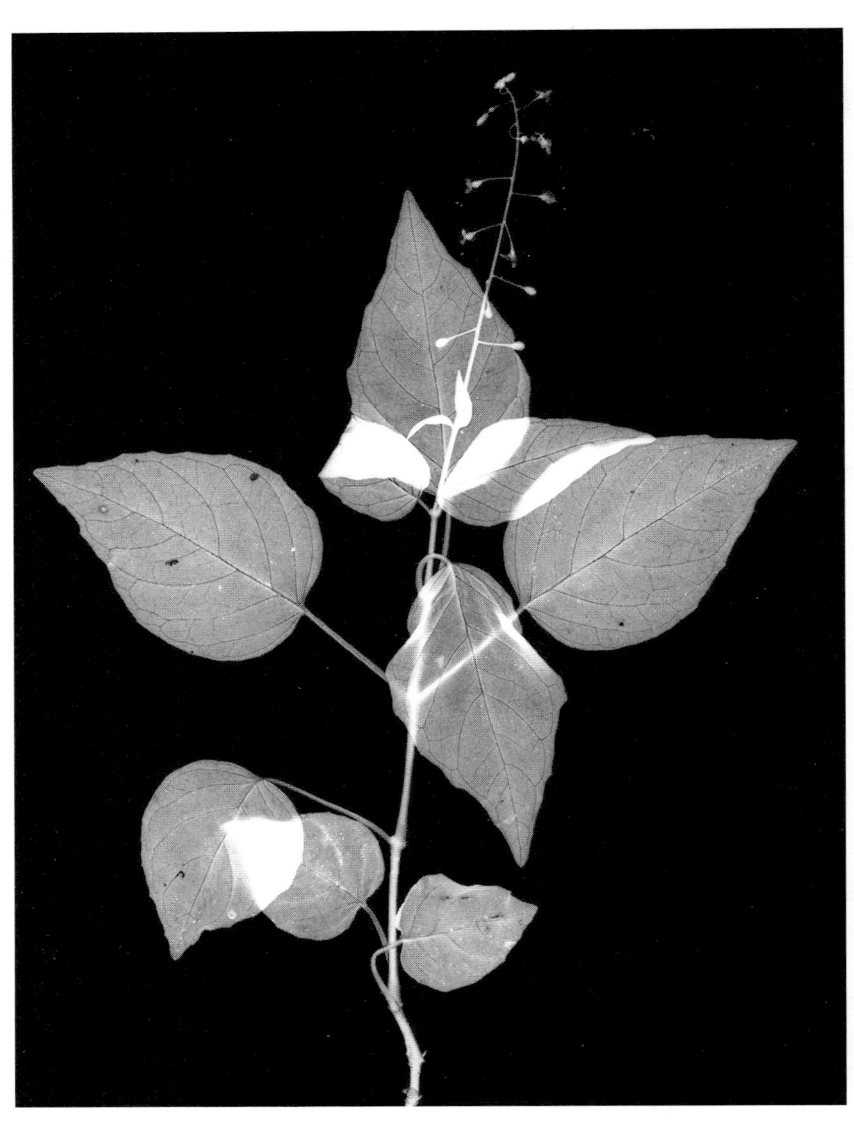

Enchanter's Nightshade
Circaea lutetiana

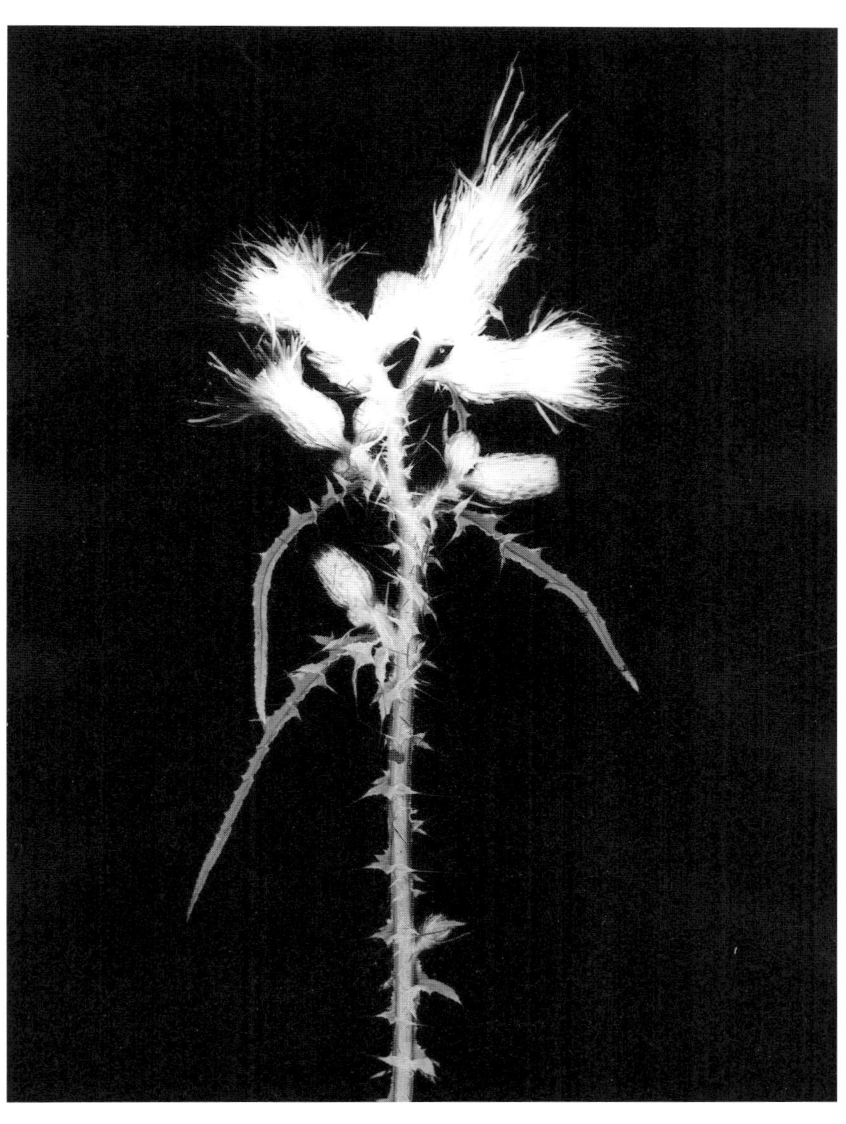

Creeping Thistle
Cirsium arvensis

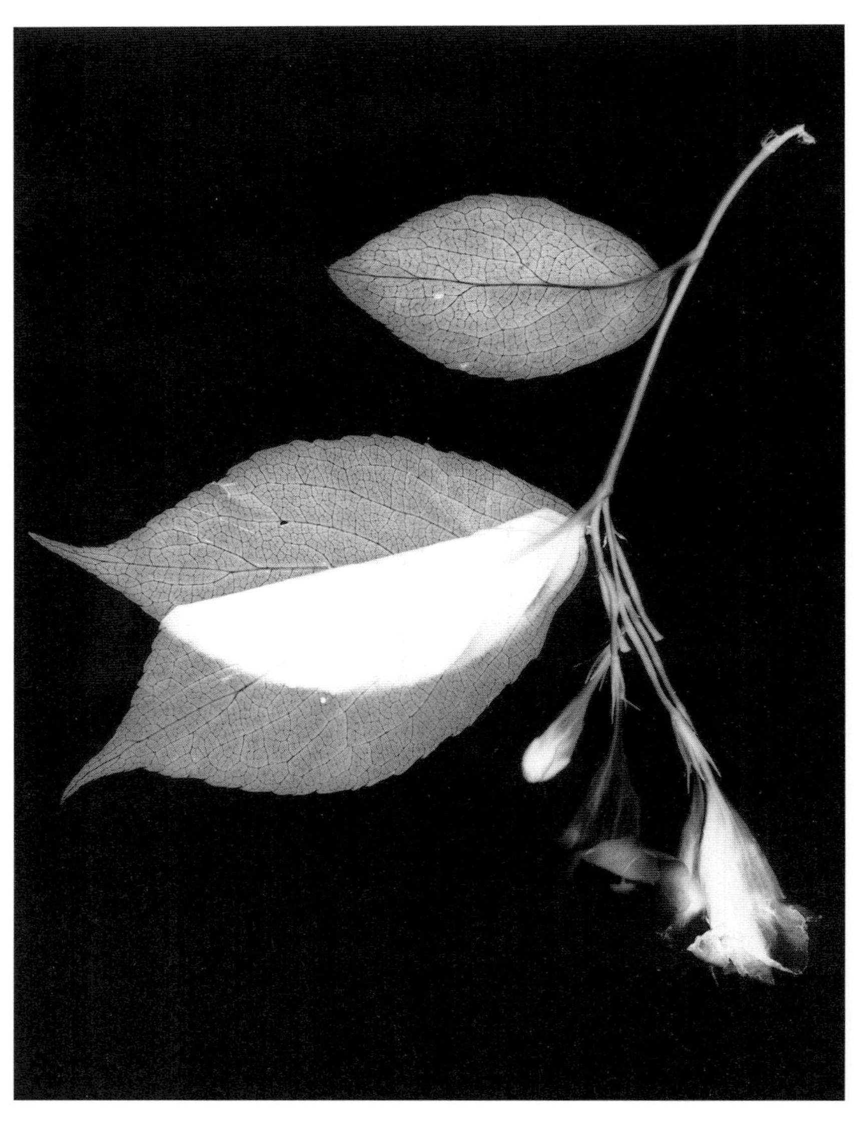

Clematis
Clematis cirrhosa

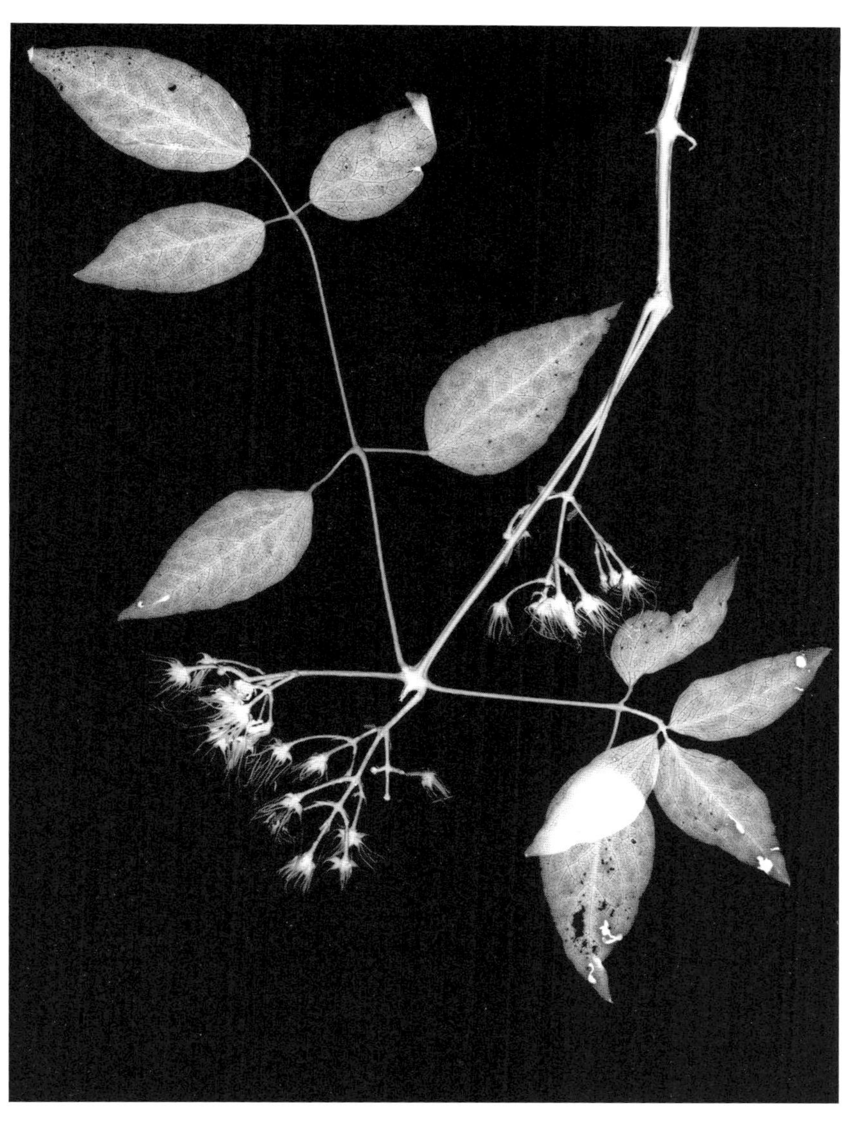

Old Man's Beard
Clematis vitalba

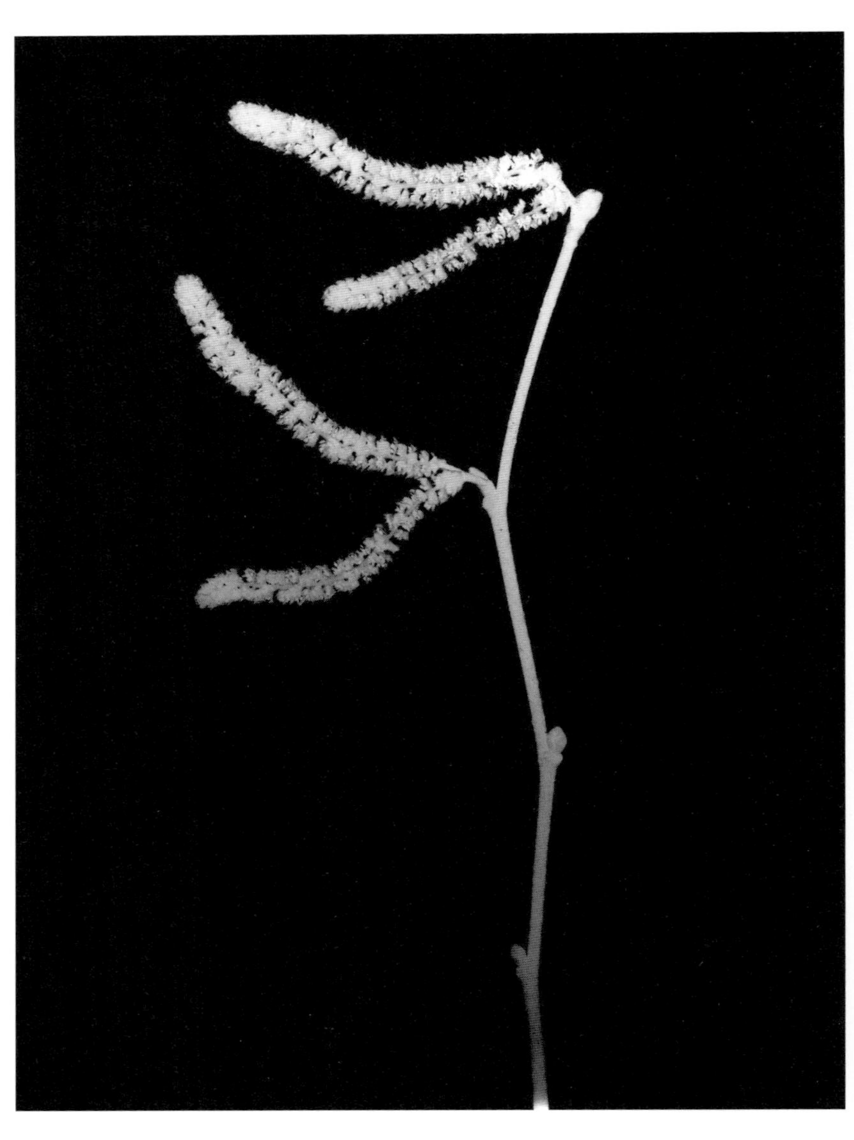

Hazel
Corylus avellana

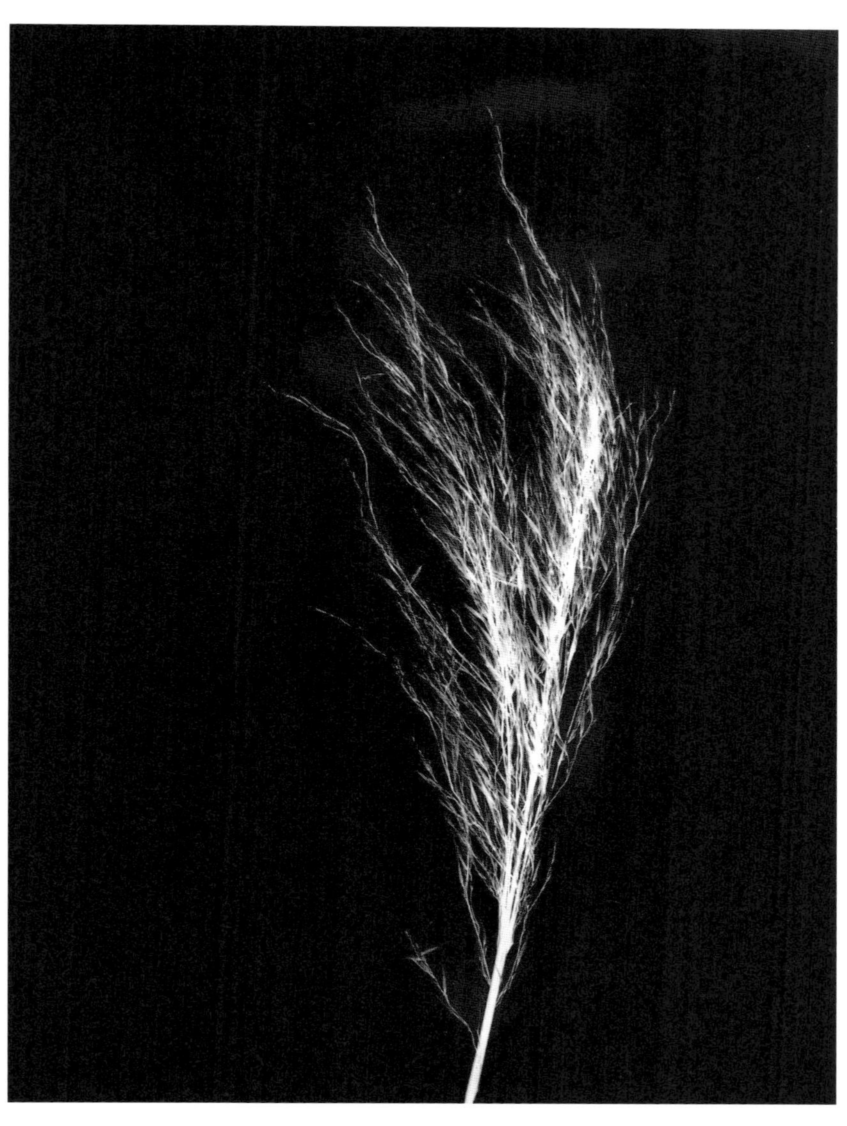

Pampas Grass
Cortaderia selloana

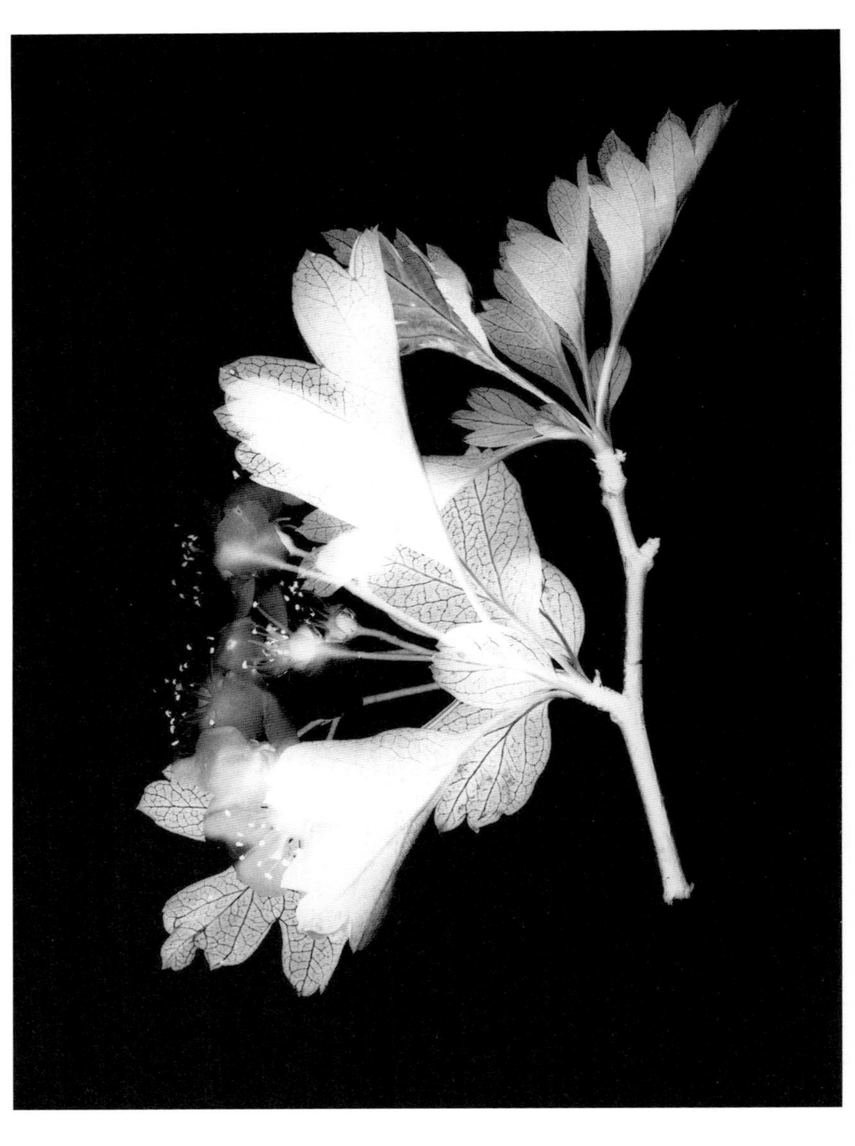

Hawthorn
Crataegus monogyna

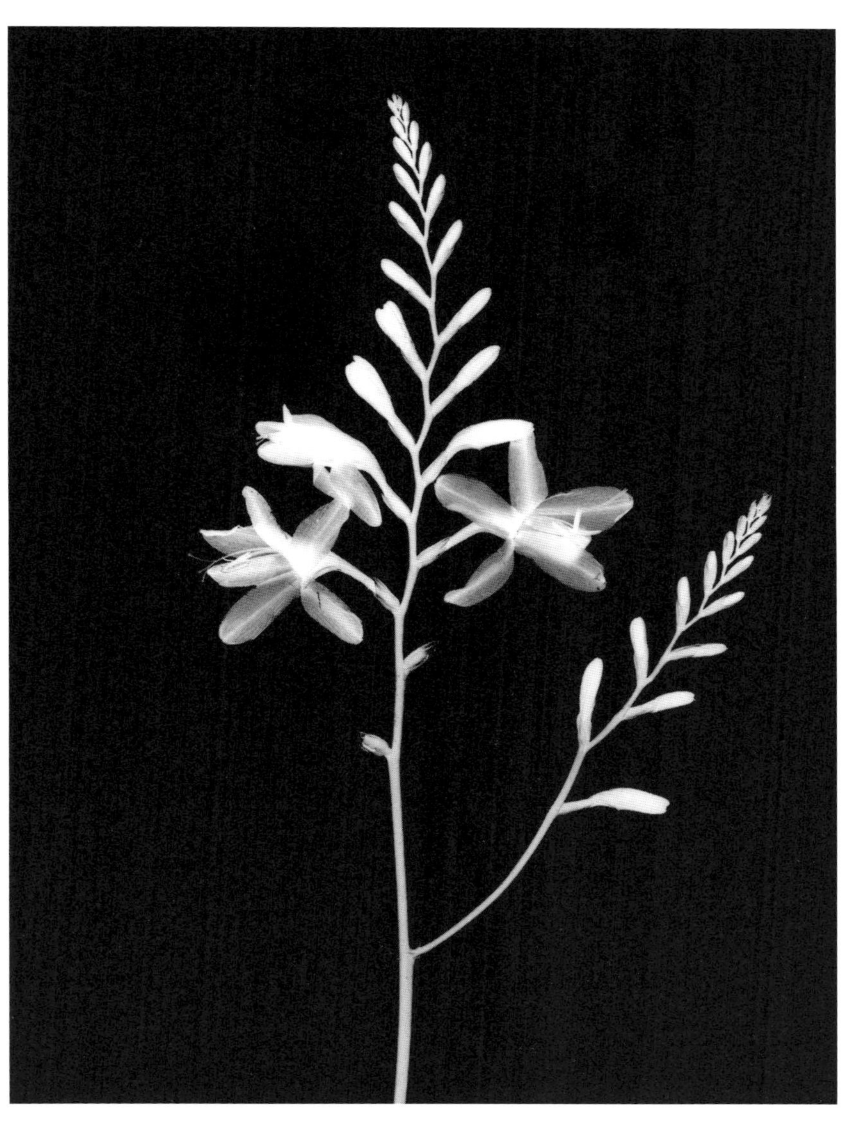

Montbretia
Crocosmia crocosmiiflora

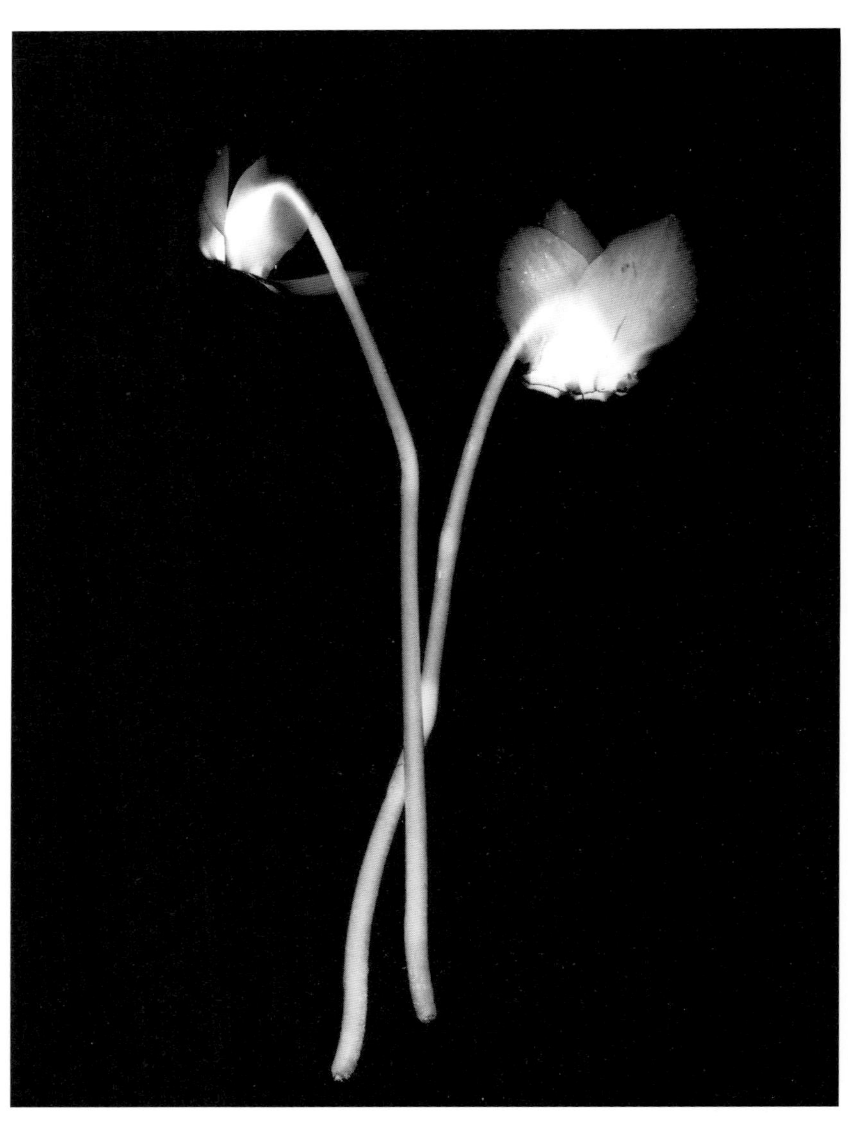

Cyclamen
Cyclamen hederifolium

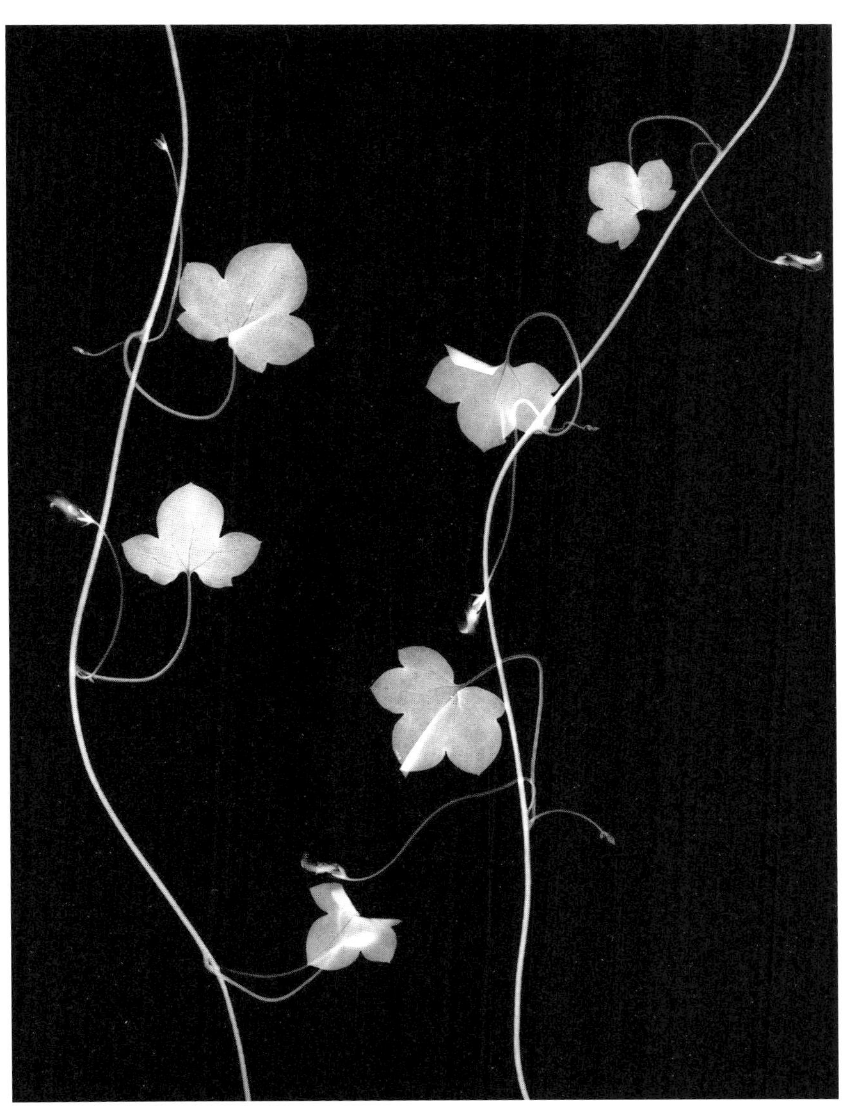

Ivy-leaved Toadflax
Cymbalaria muralis

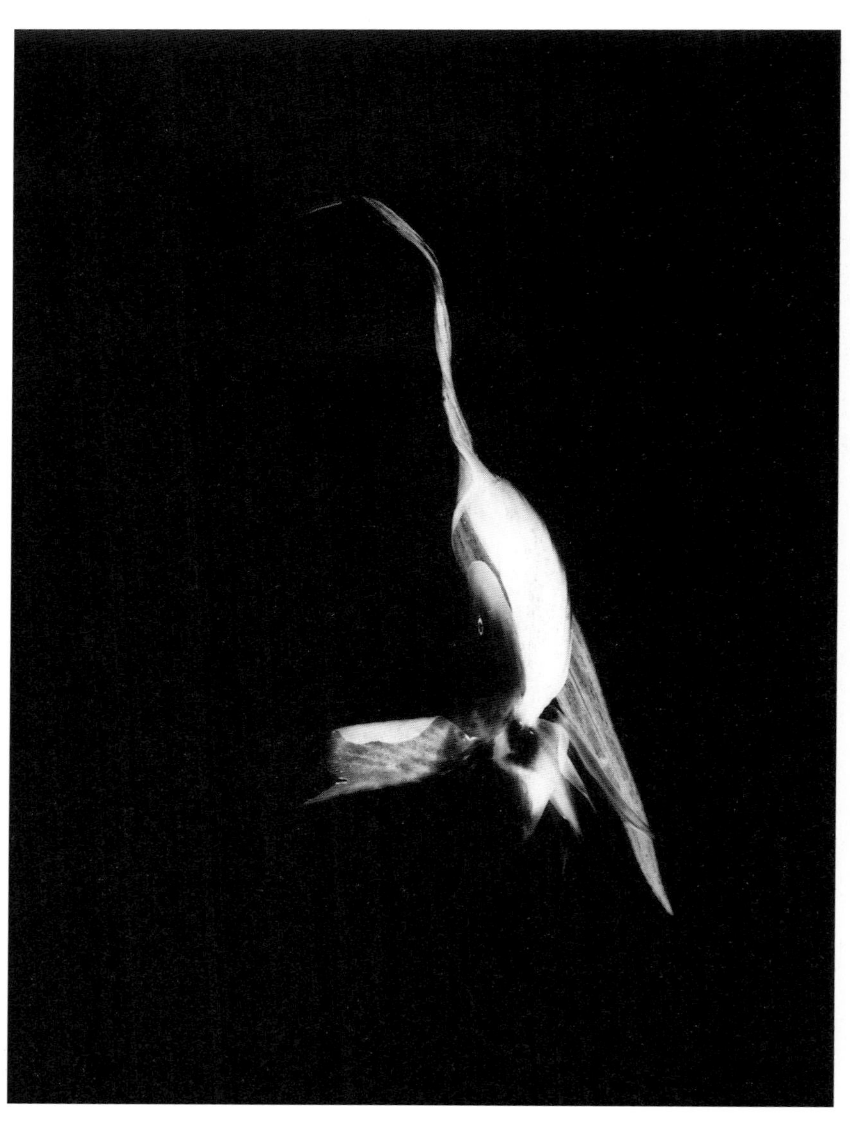

Southern Marsh Orchid
Dactylorhiza praetermissa

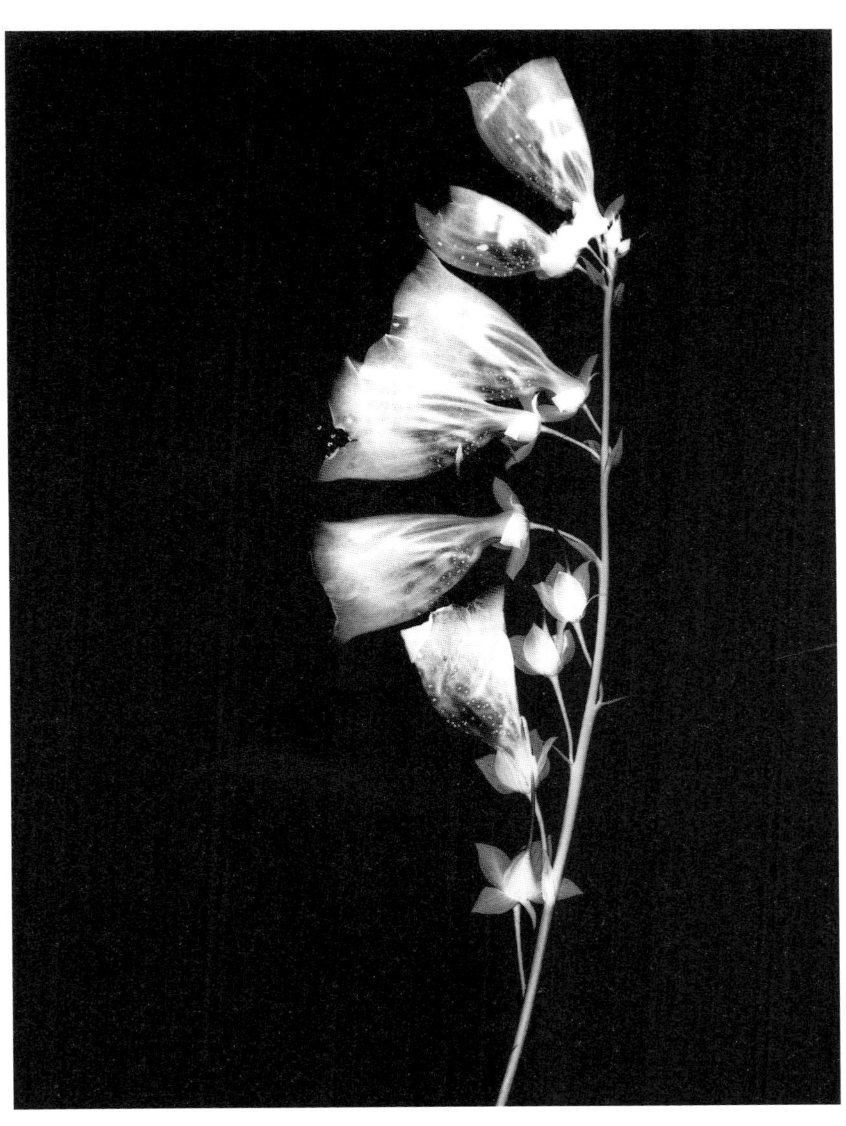

Foxglove
Digitalis purpurea

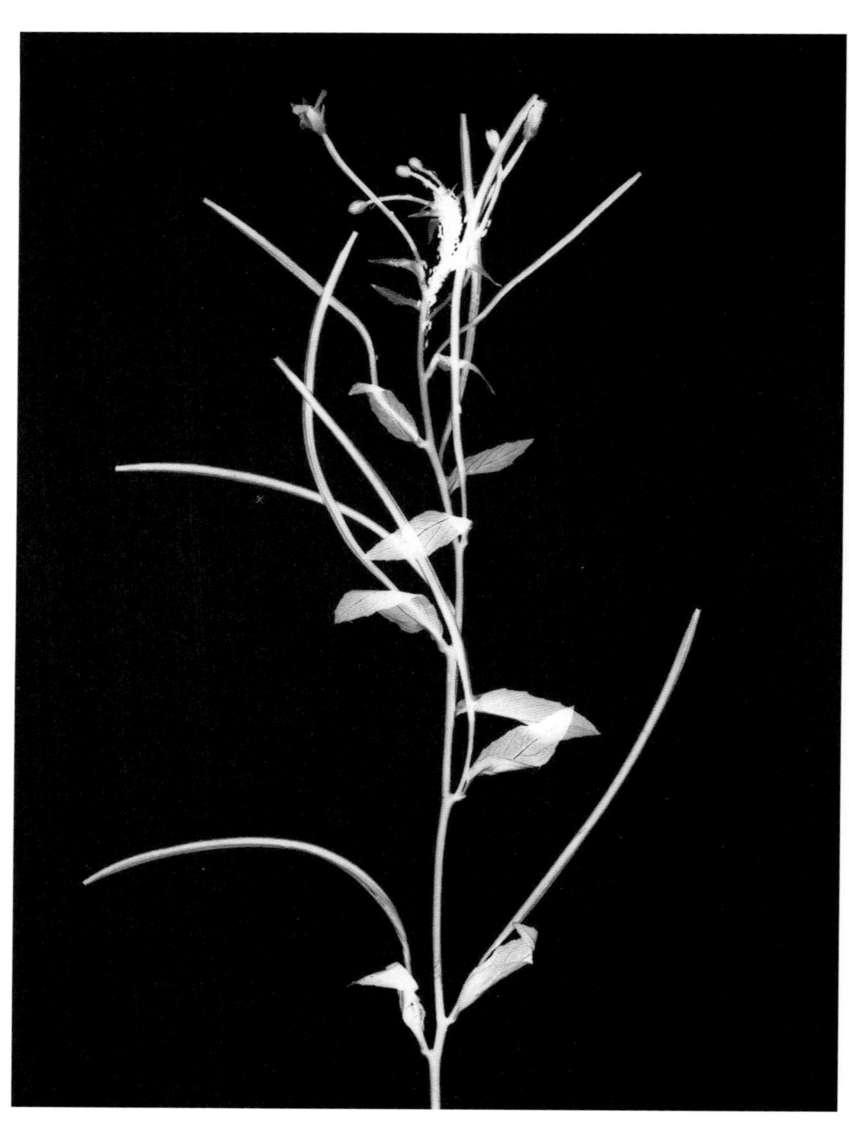

Hoary Willowherb
Epilobium parvifolium

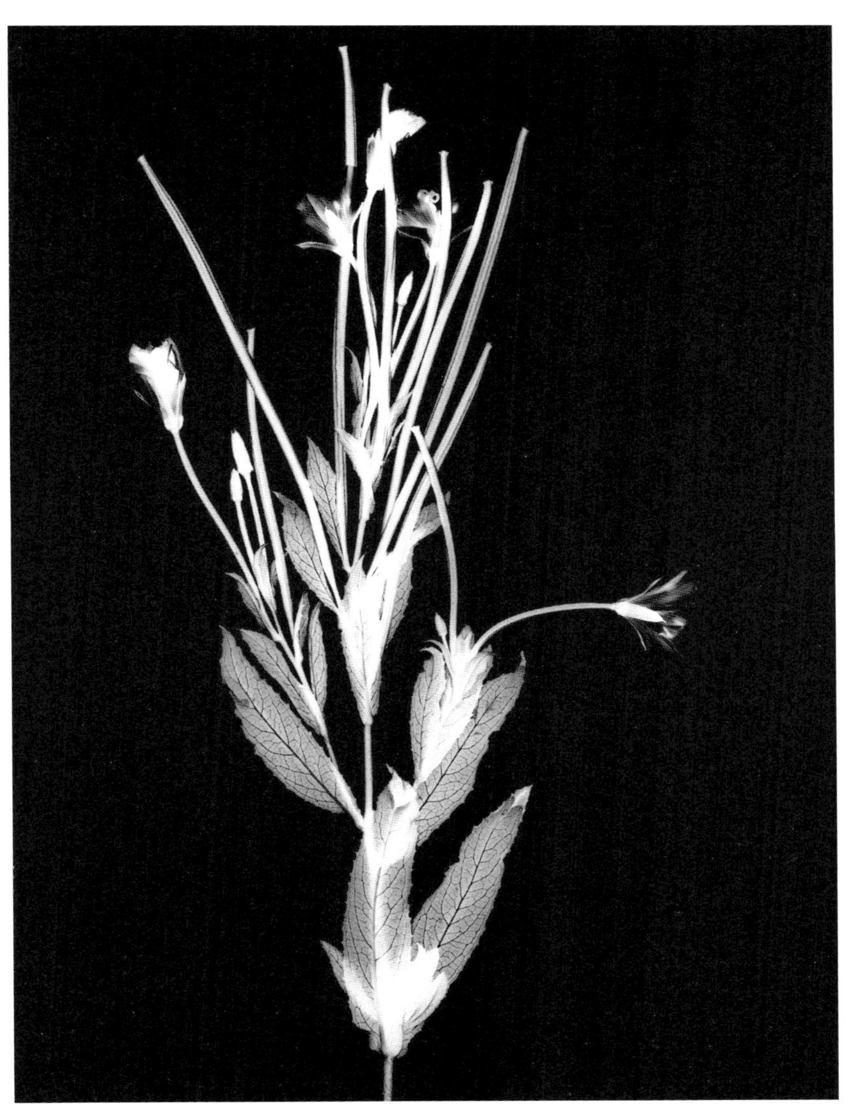

Great Willowherb
Epilobium hirsutum

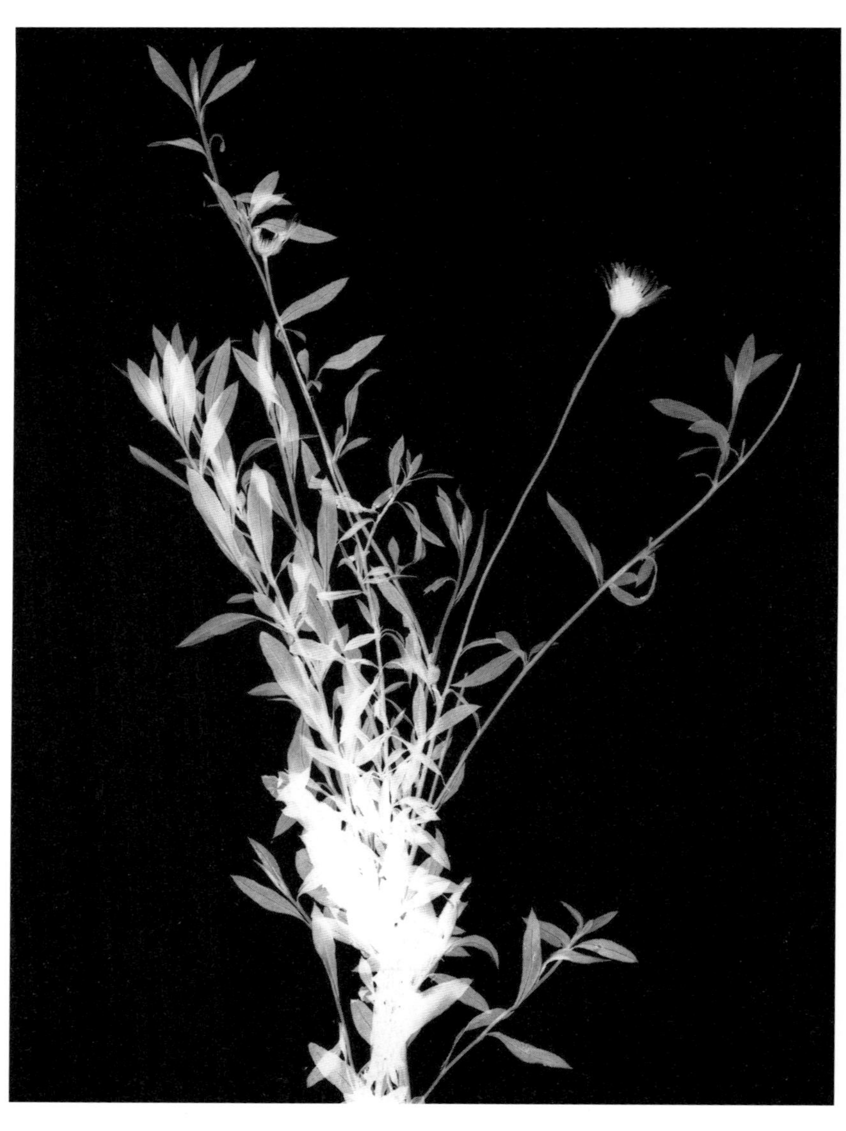

Santa Barbara Daisy
Erigeron karvinskianus

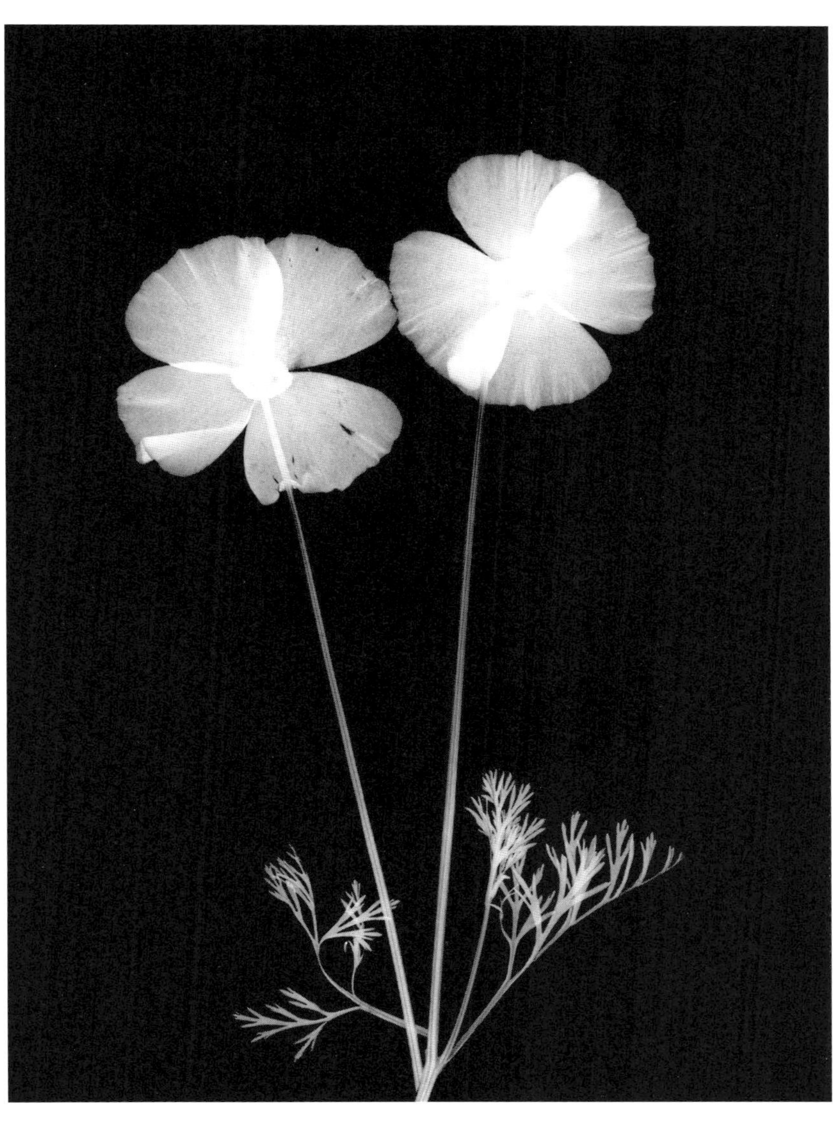

California Poppy
Eschscholzia californica

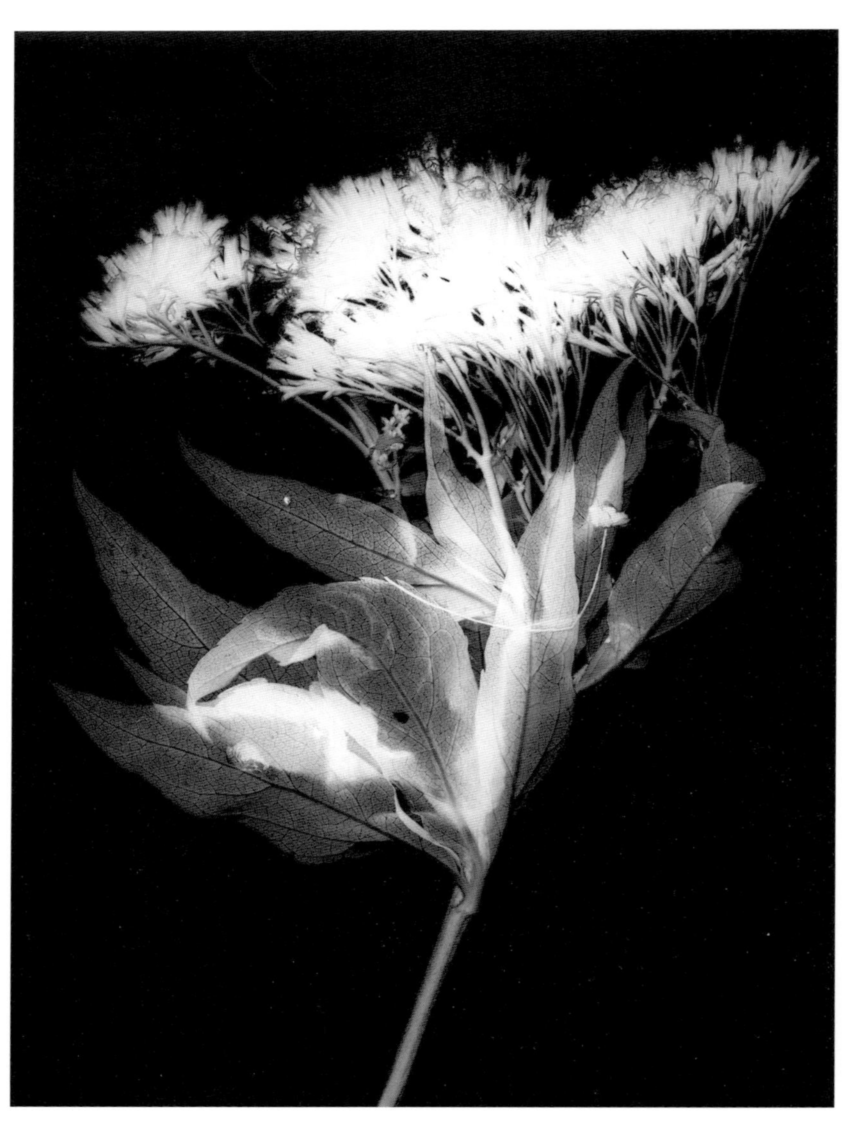

Joe-Pye Weed
Eutrochium purpureum

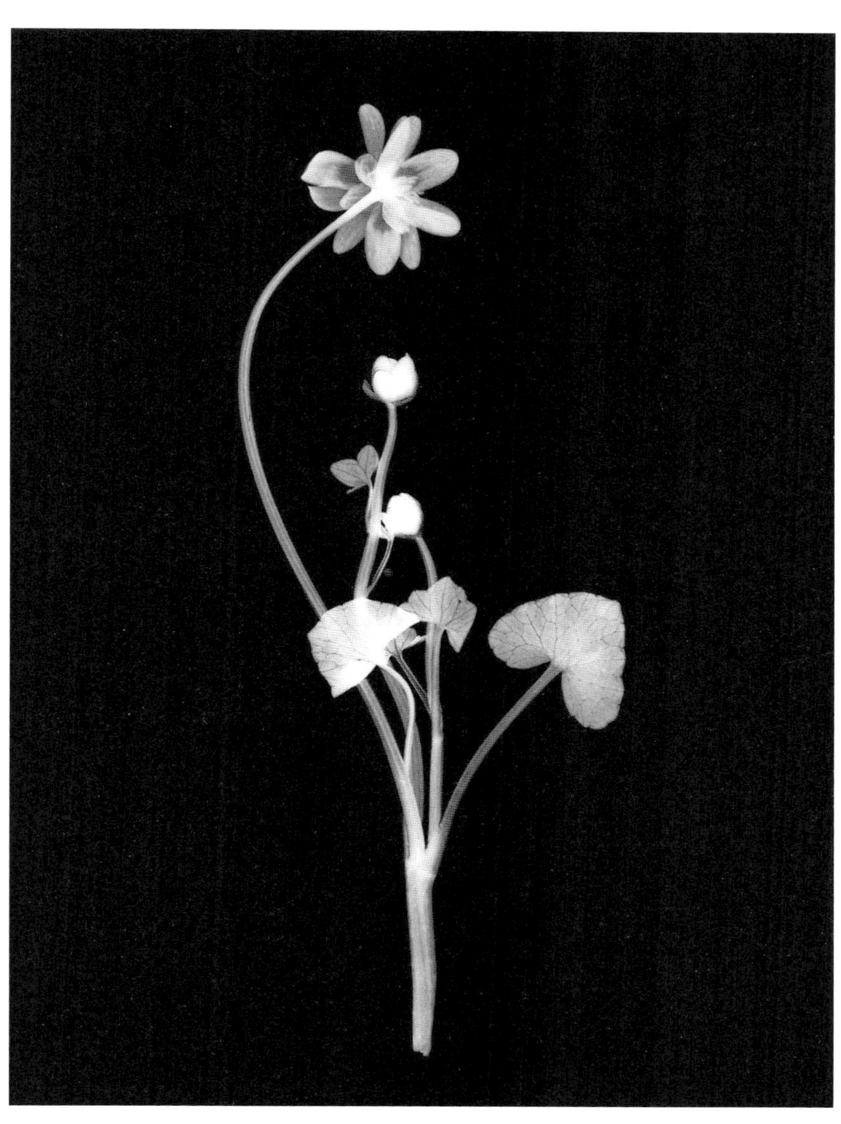

Celandine
Ficaria verna

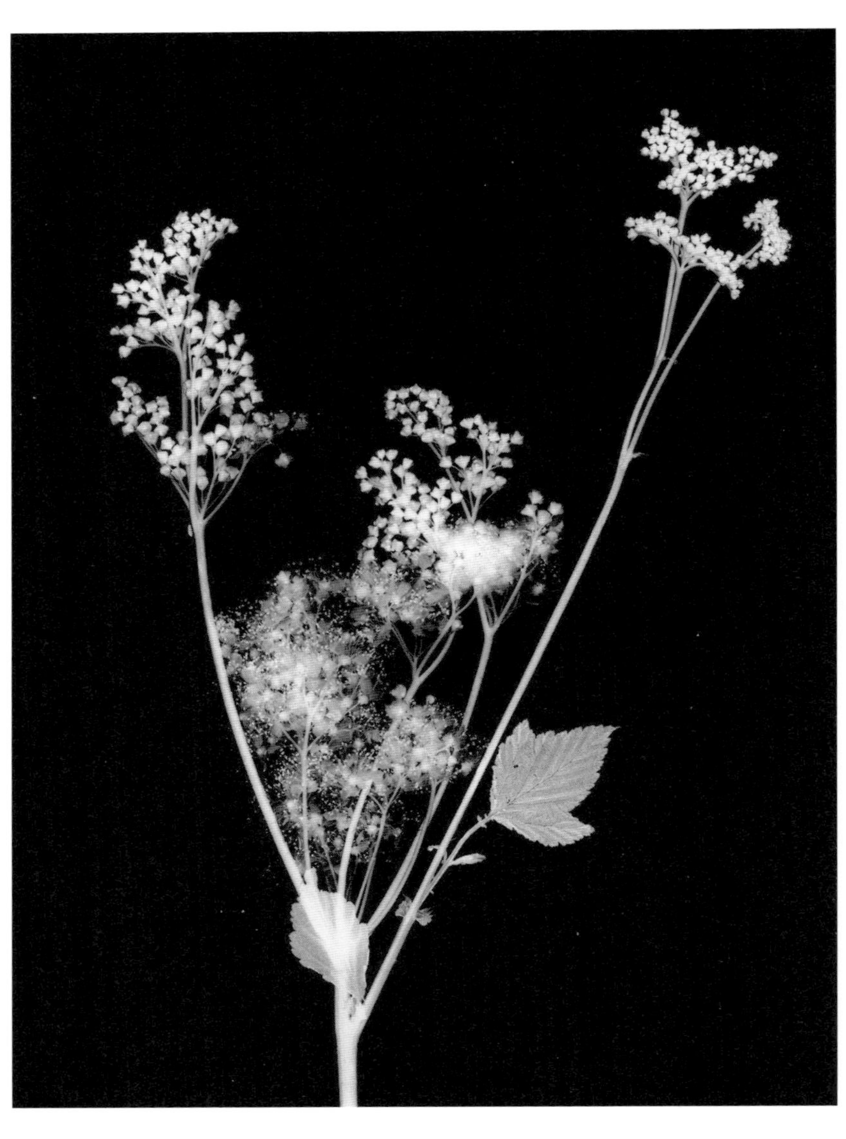

Meadowsweet
Filipendula ulmaria

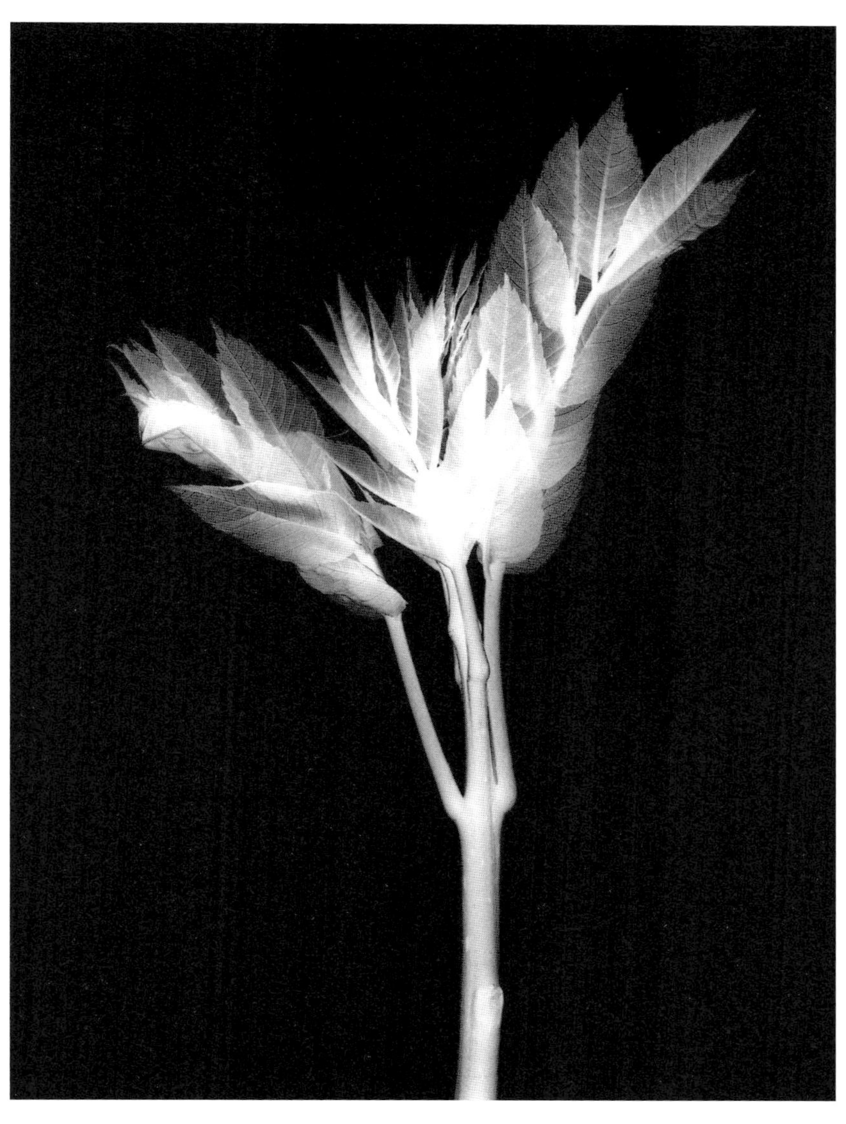

Ash
Fraxinus excelsior

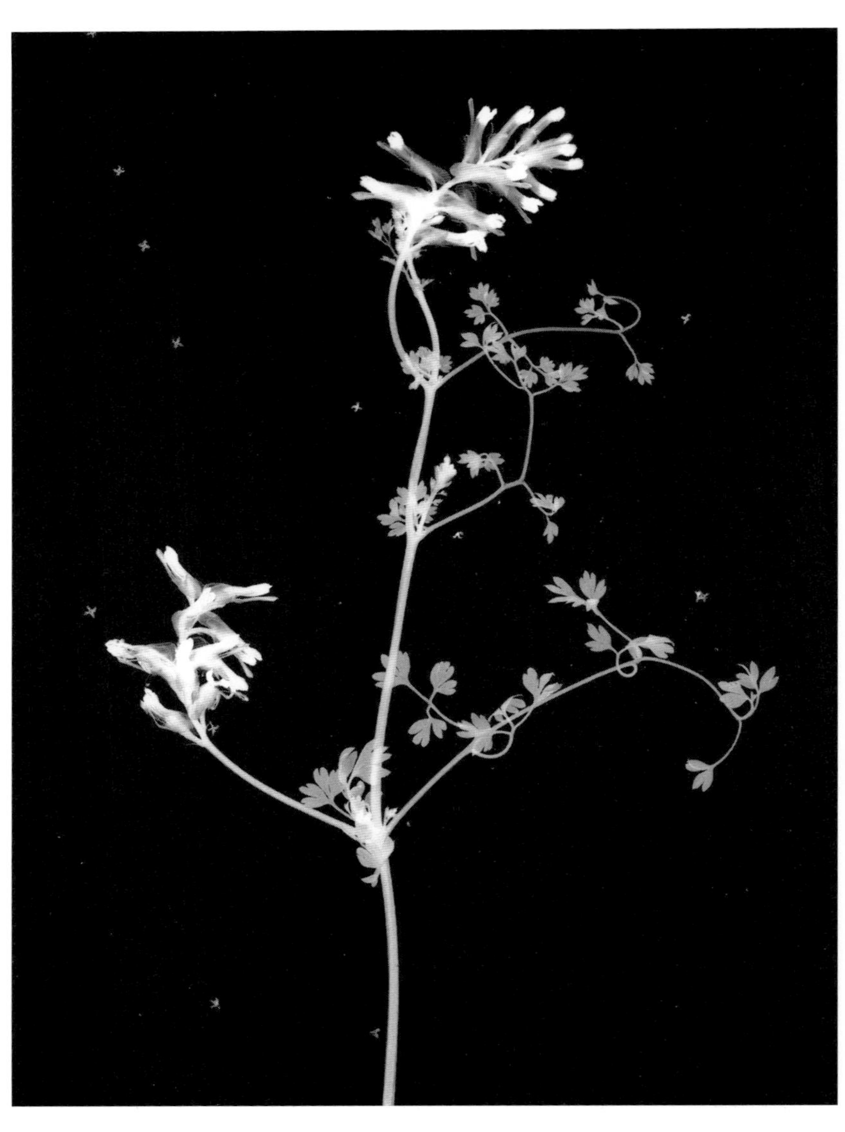

Fumatory
Fumaria officinalis

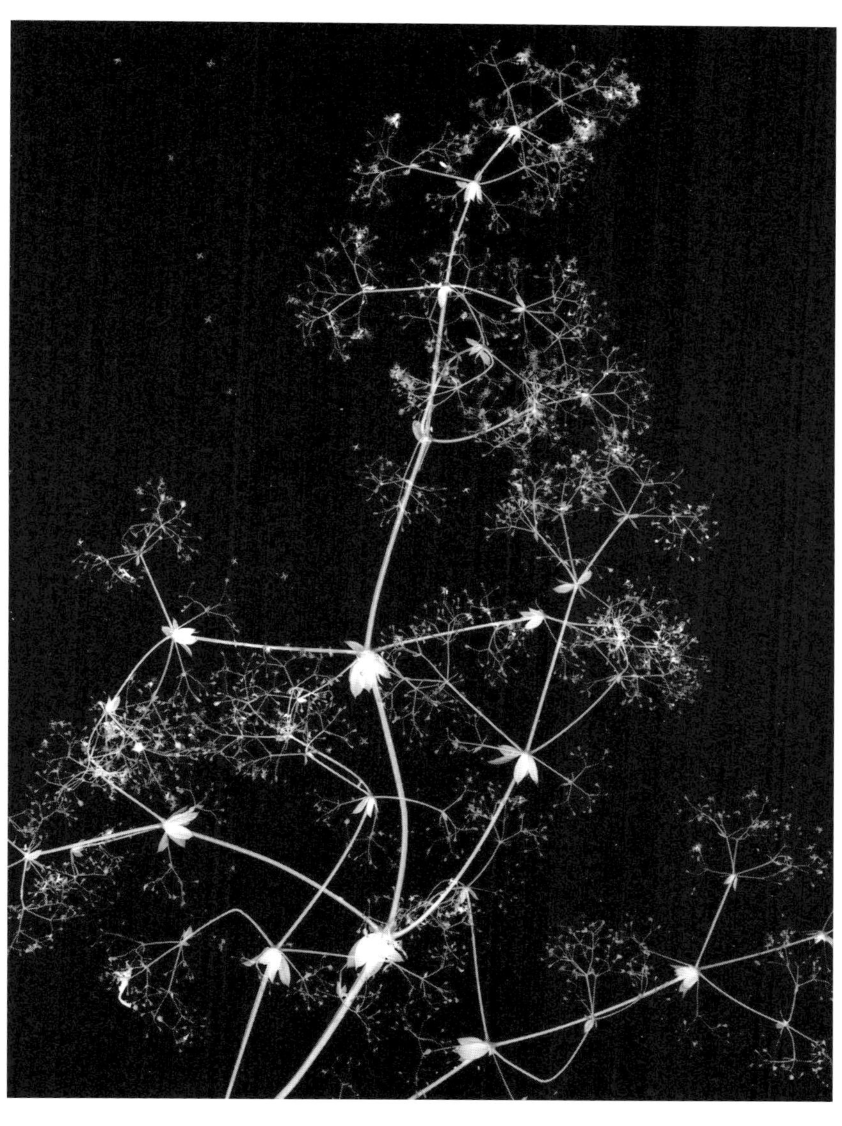

Hedge Bedstraw
Galium album

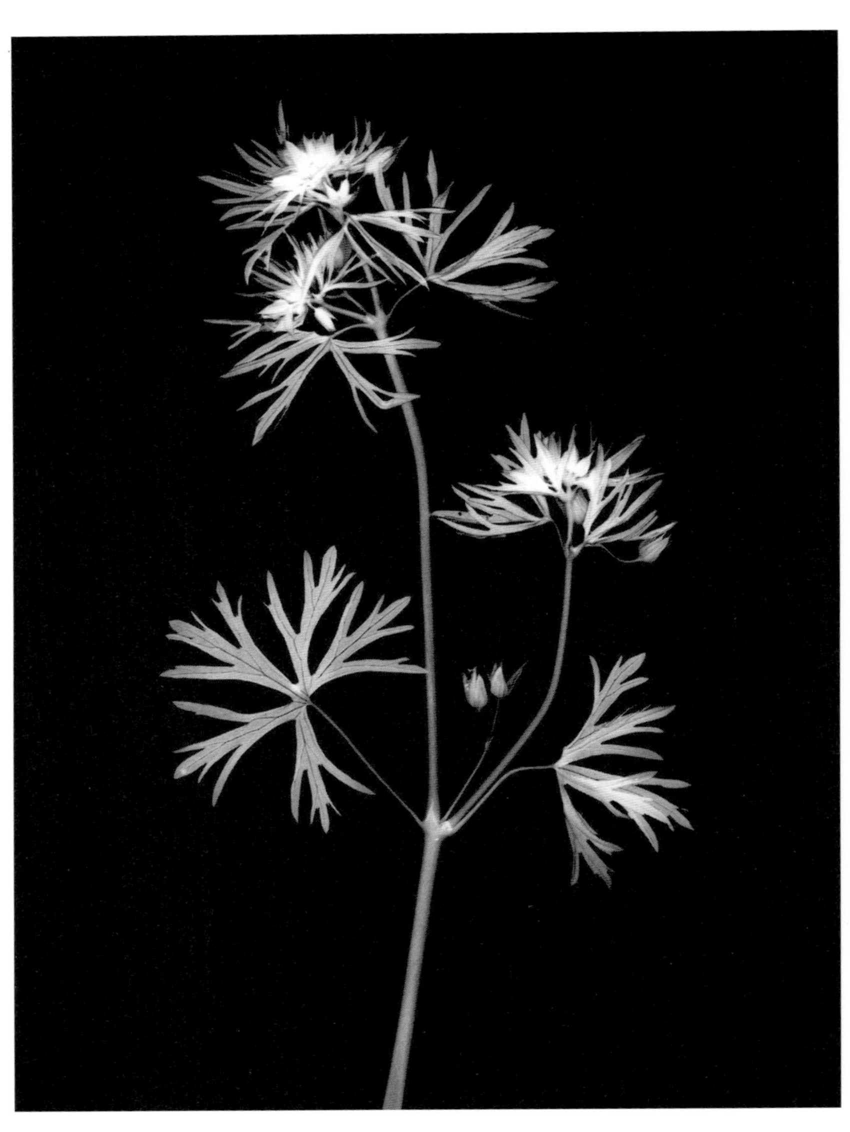

Cut-leaved Crane's-bill
Geranium dissectum

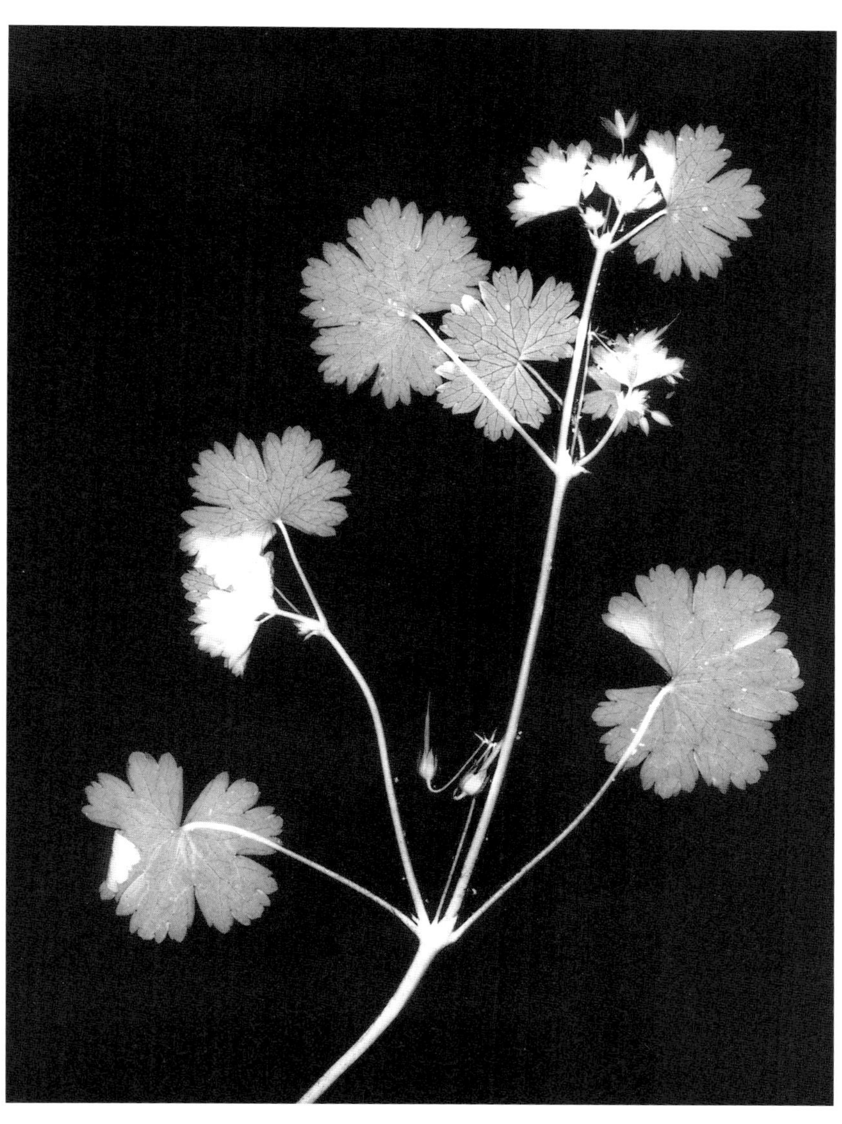

Shining Speedwell
Geranium lucidum

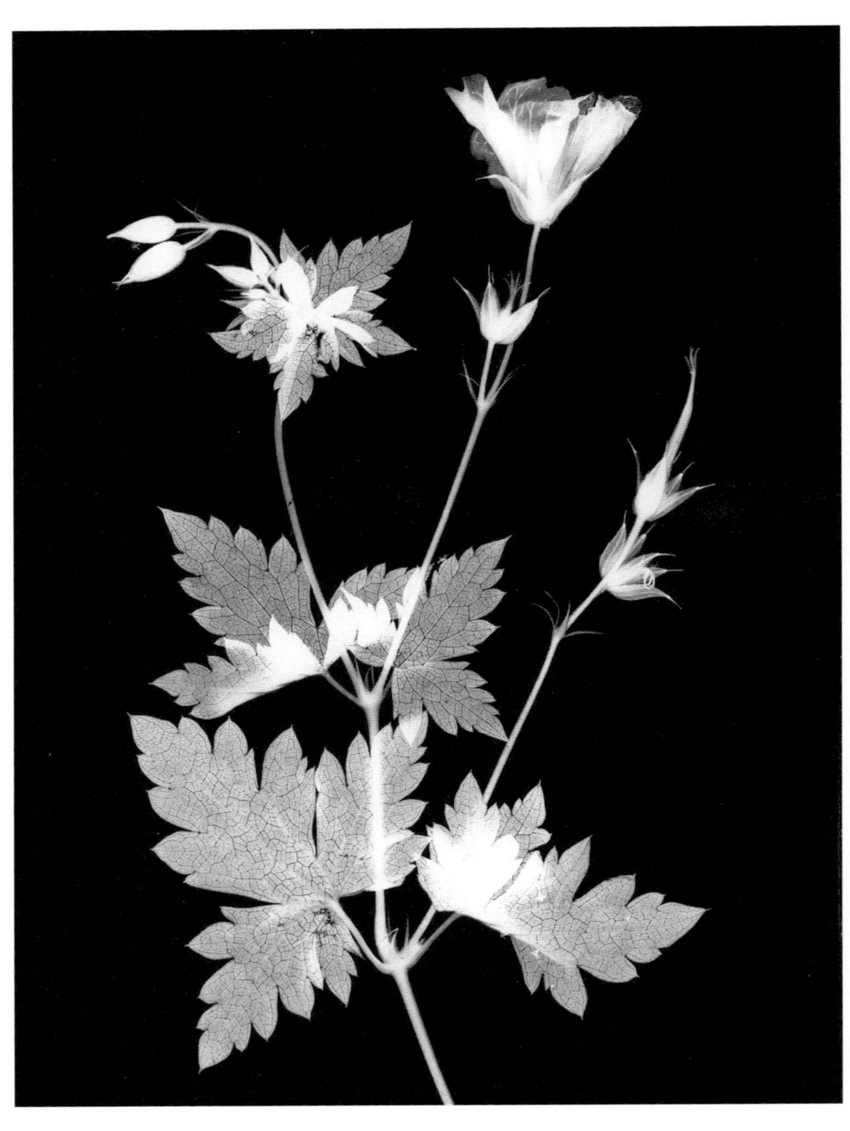

Geranium
Geranium oxonianium

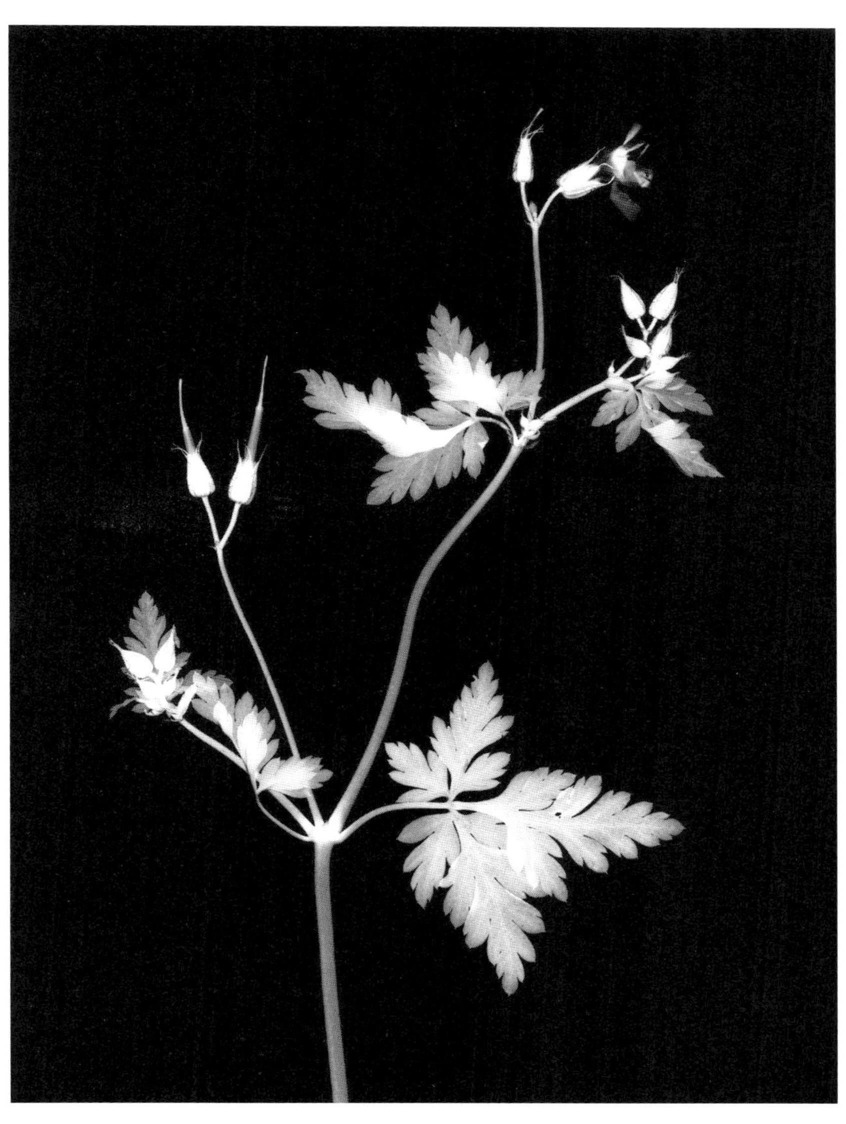

Herb Robert
Geranium robertianum

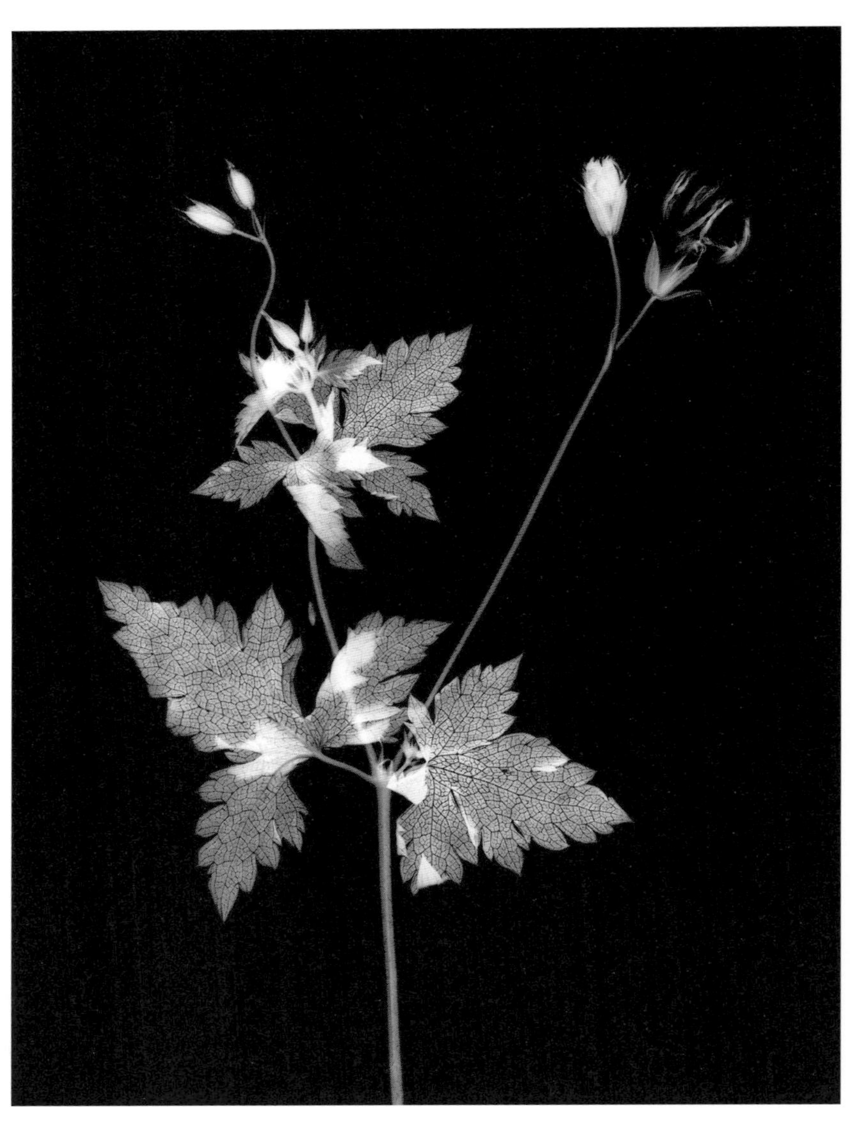

Wood Crane's-bill
Geranium sylvaticum

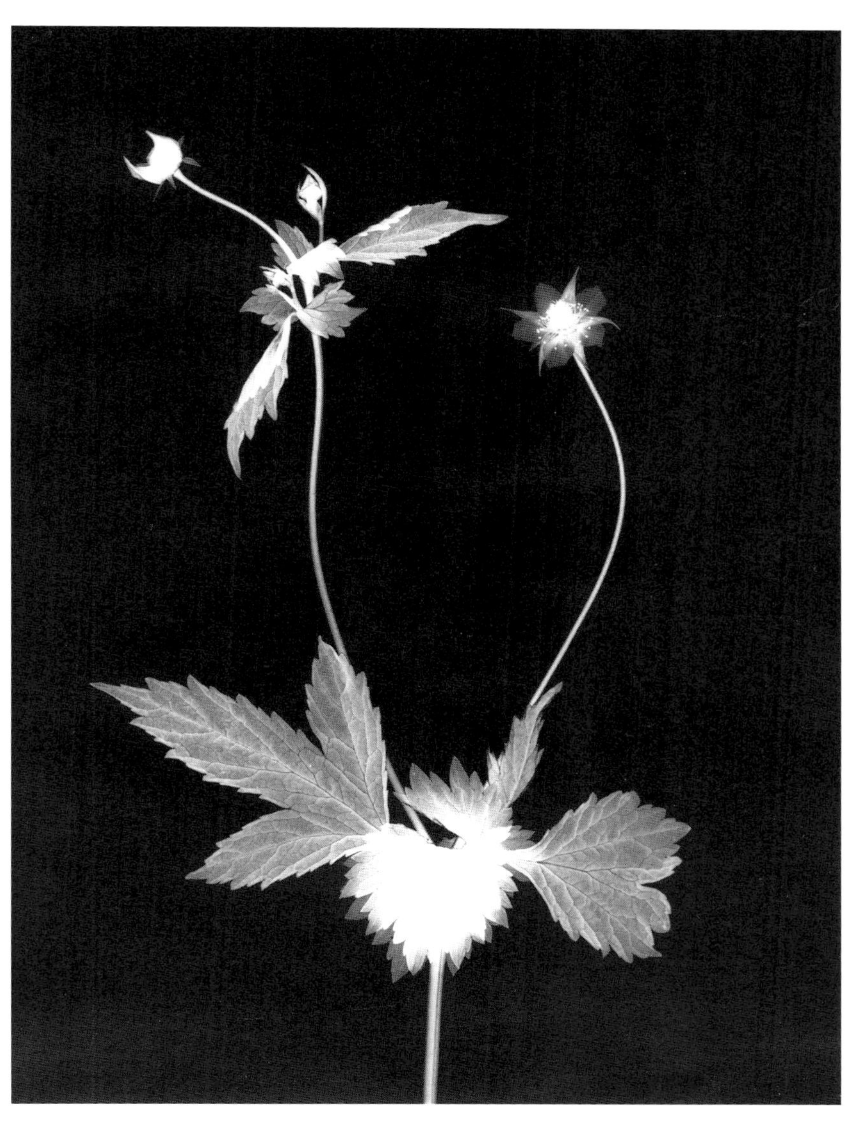

Herb Bennet
Geum urbanum

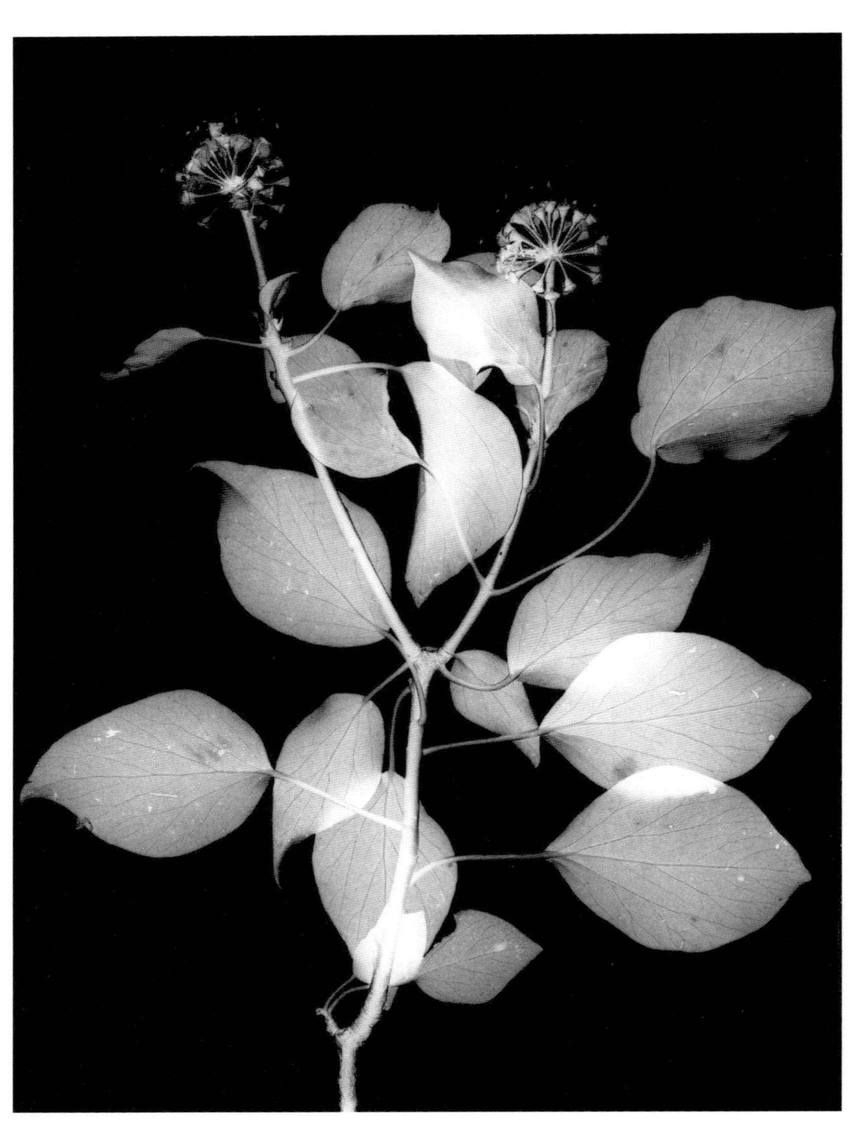

European Ivy
Hedera helix

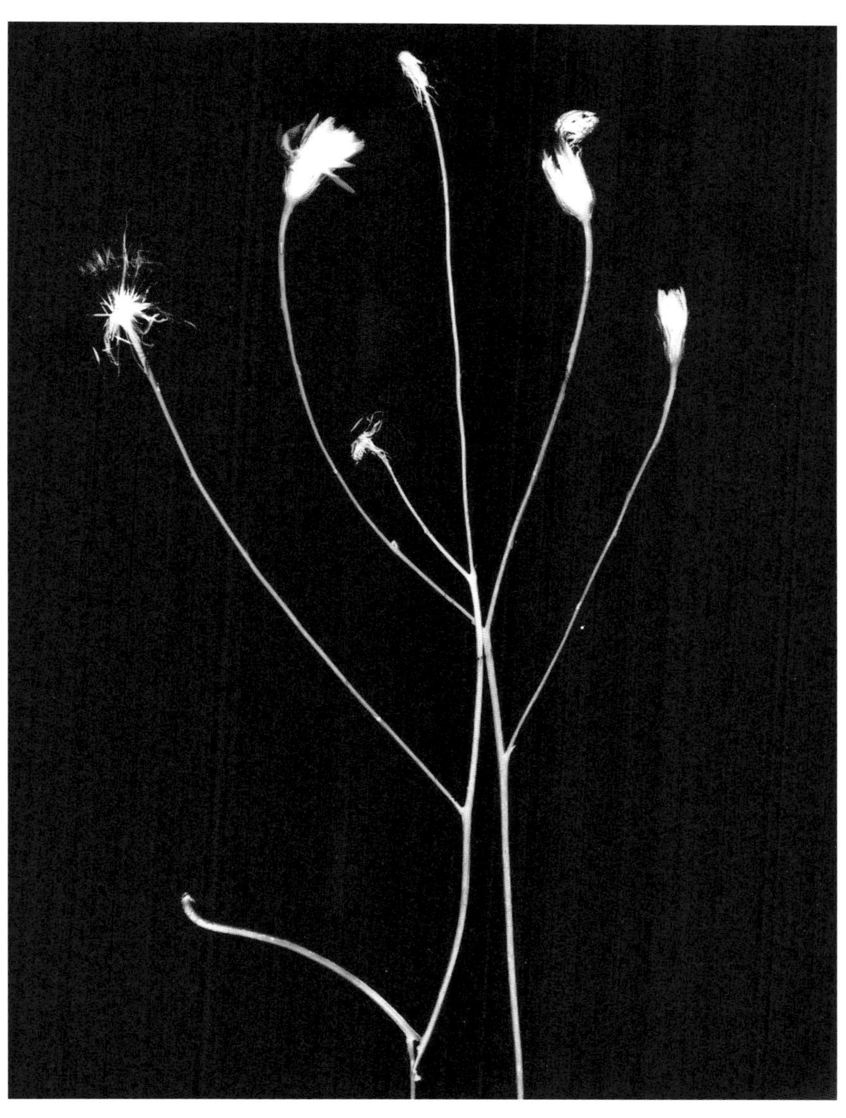

Common Hawkweed
Hieracium caespitosum

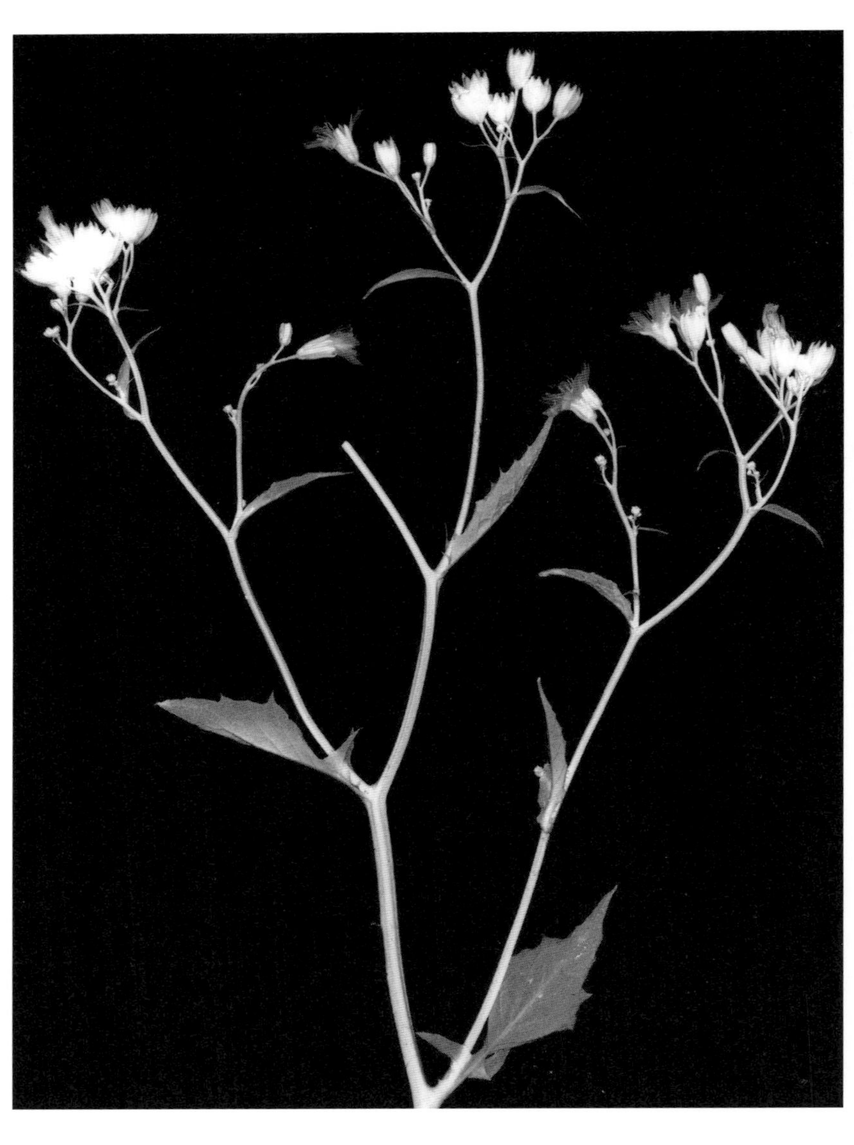

Meadow Hawkweed
Hieracium pratense

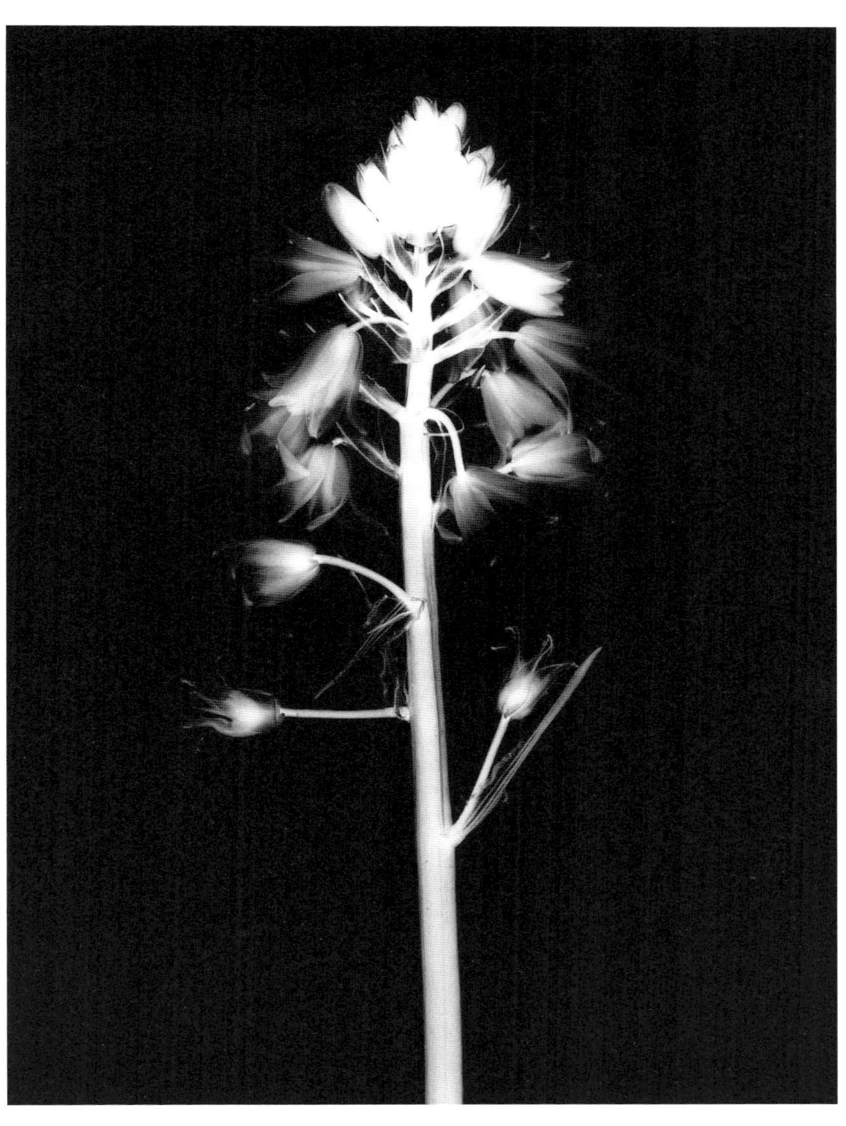

Spanish Bluebell
Hyacinthoides hispanica

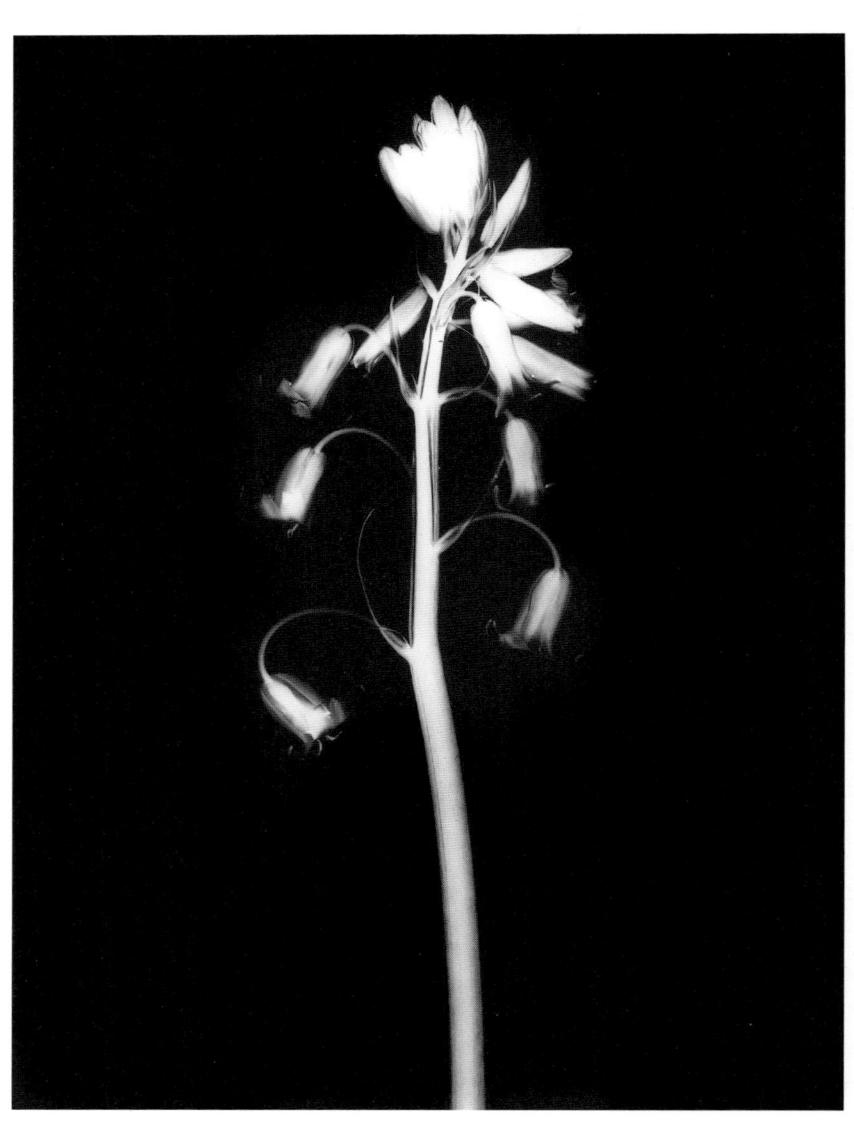

Hybrid Bluebell
Hyacinthoides non-scripta x hispanica

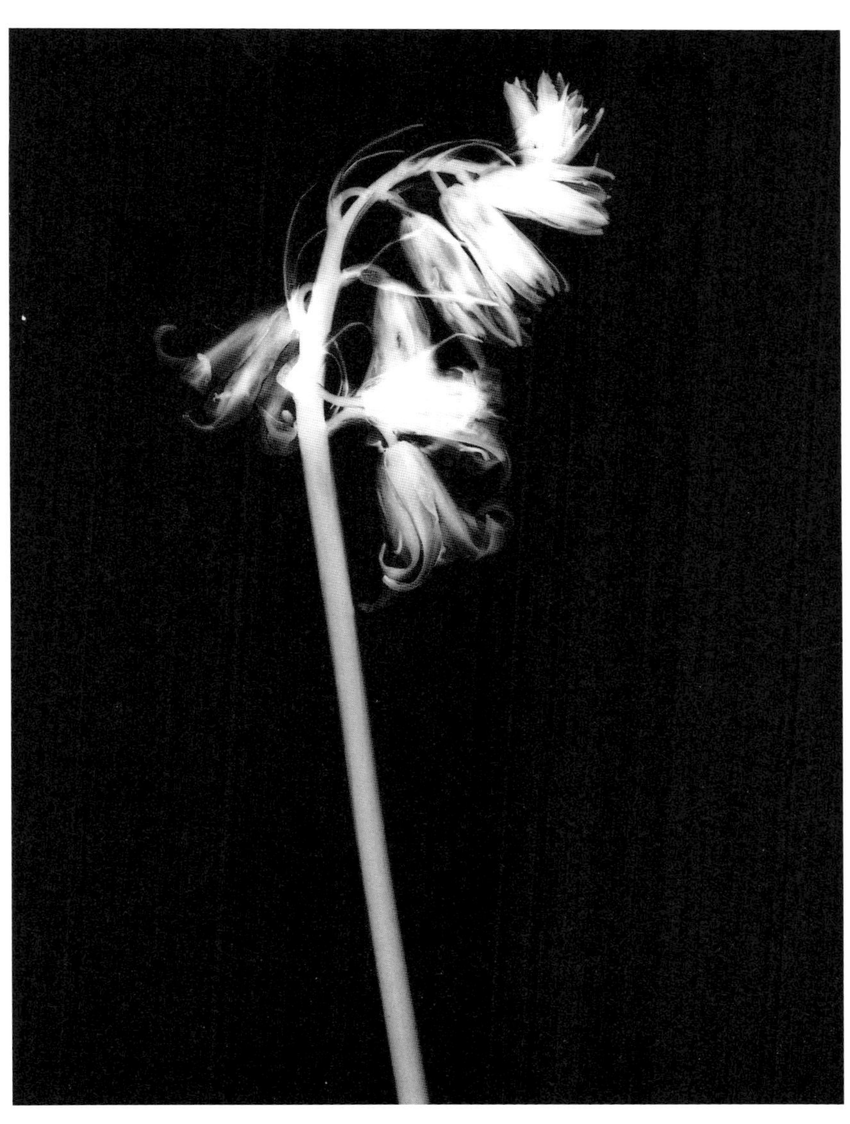

English Bluebell
Hyacinthoides non-scripta

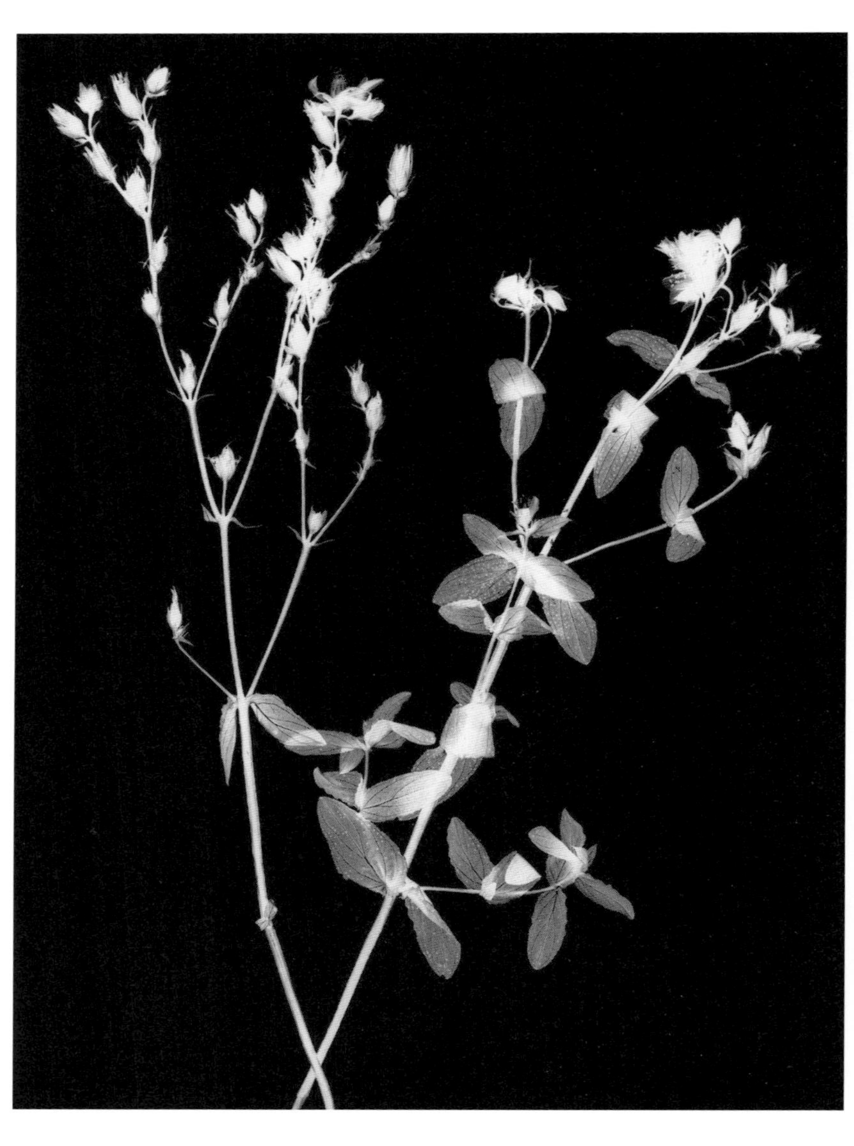

Slender St John's Wort
Hypericum pulchrum

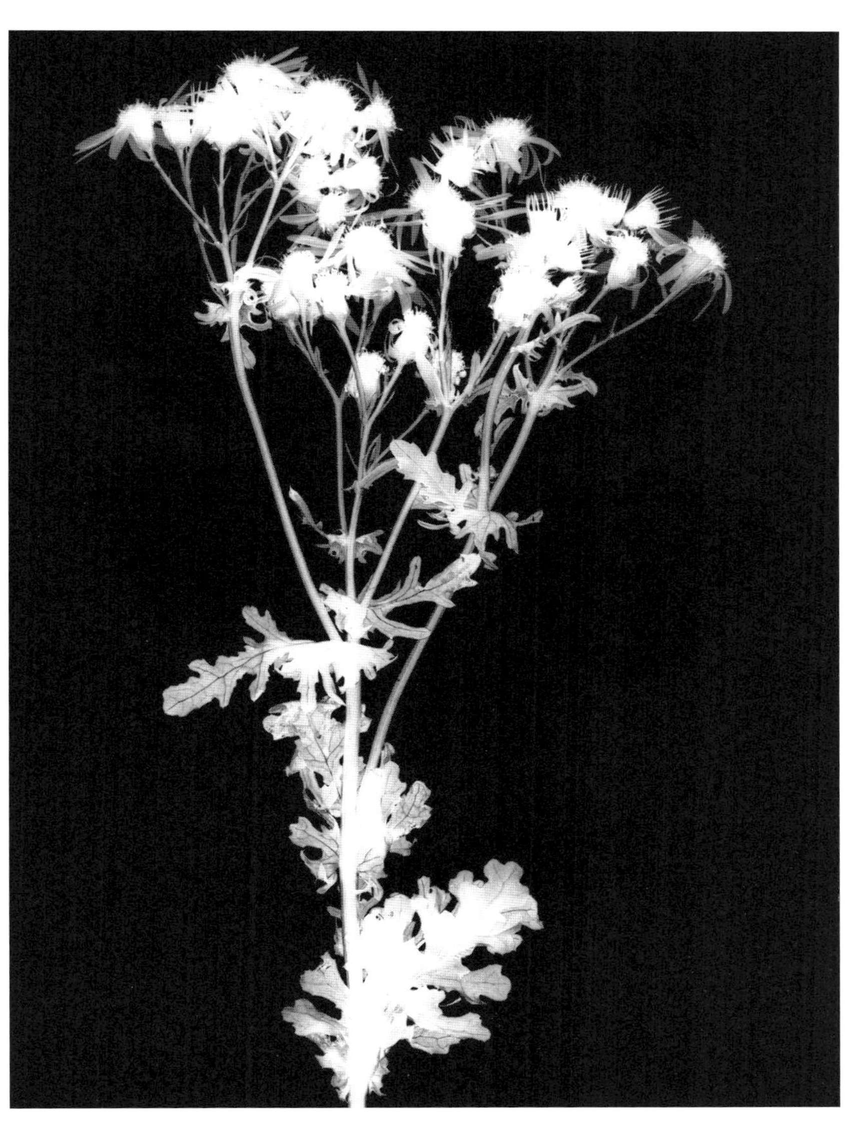

Ragwort
Jacobaea vulgaris

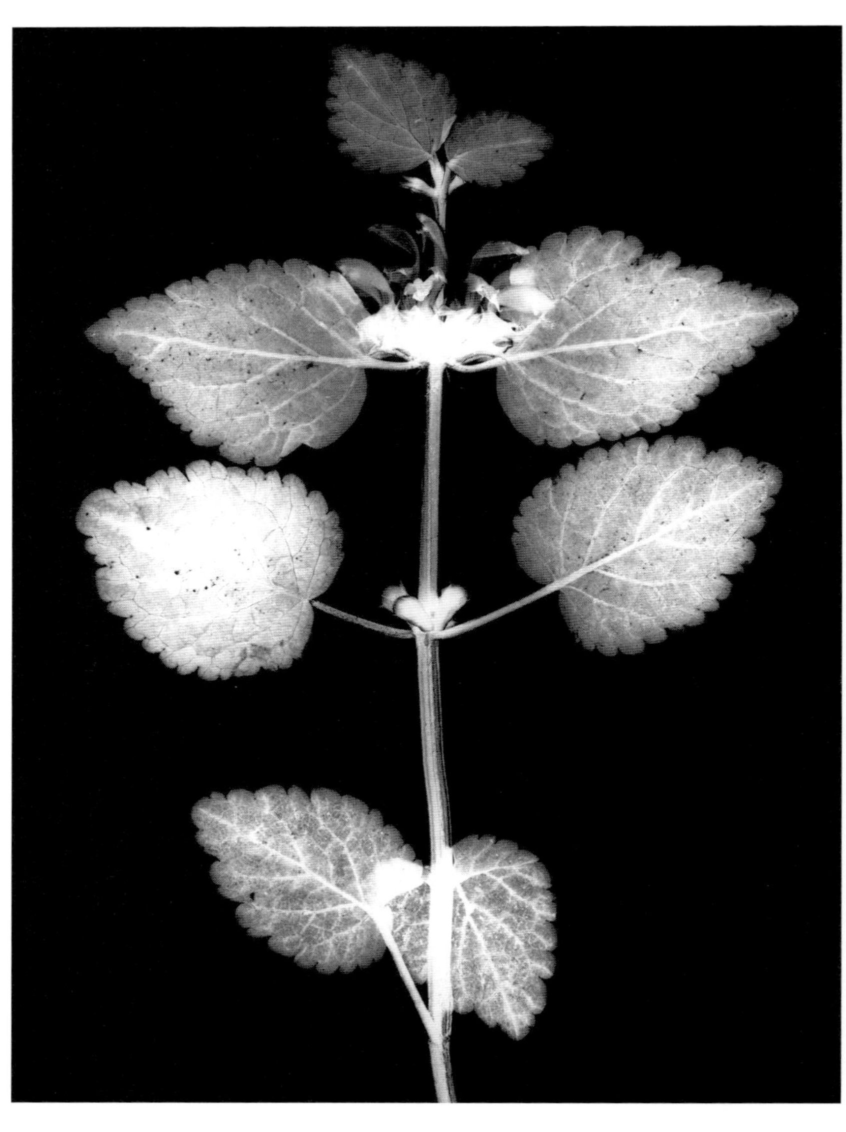

Yellow Archangel

Lamium galeobdolon

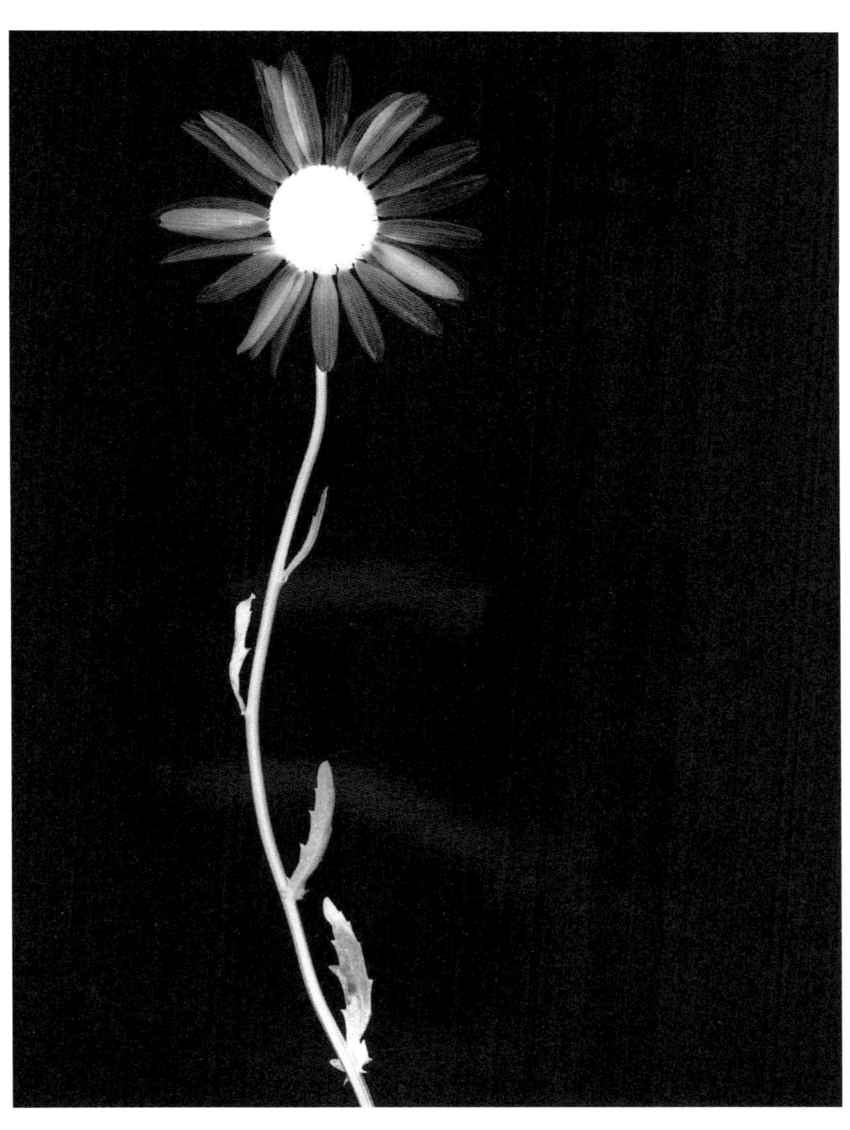

Ox-eye Daisy
Leucanthemum vulgare

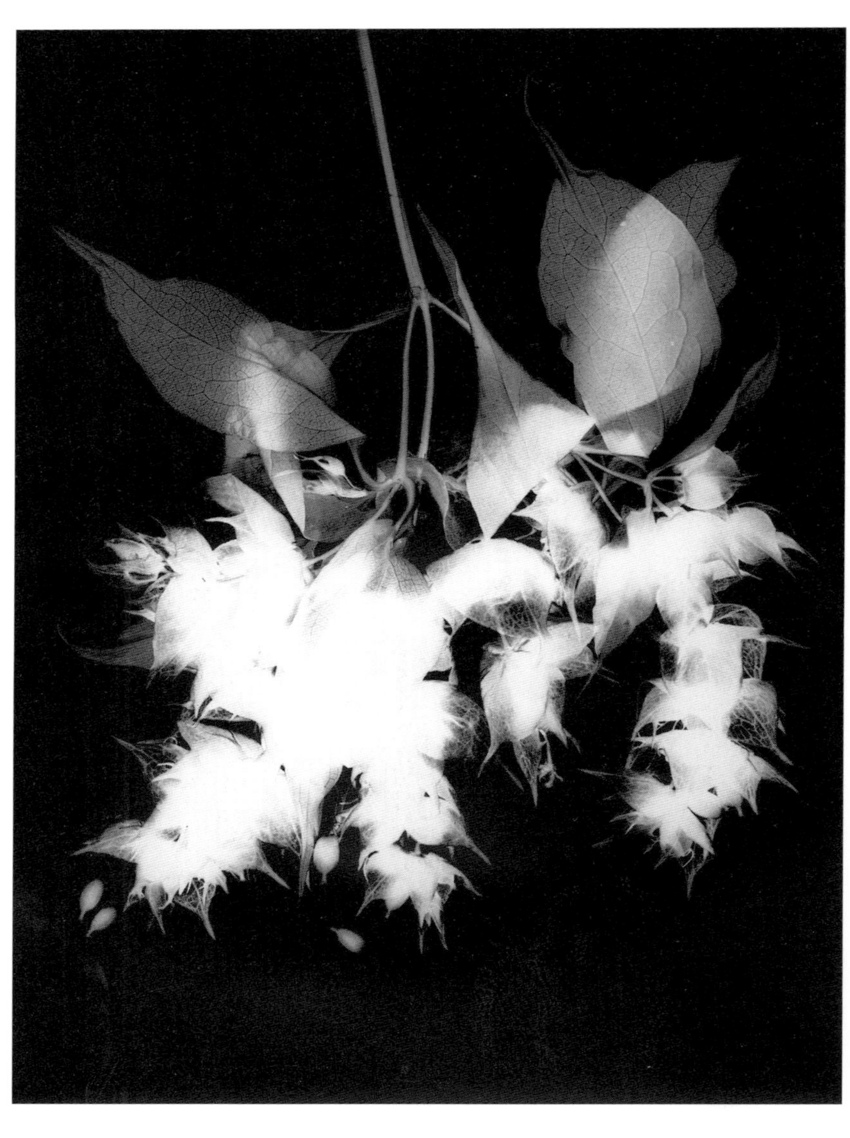

Himalayan Honeysuckle
Leycesteria formosa

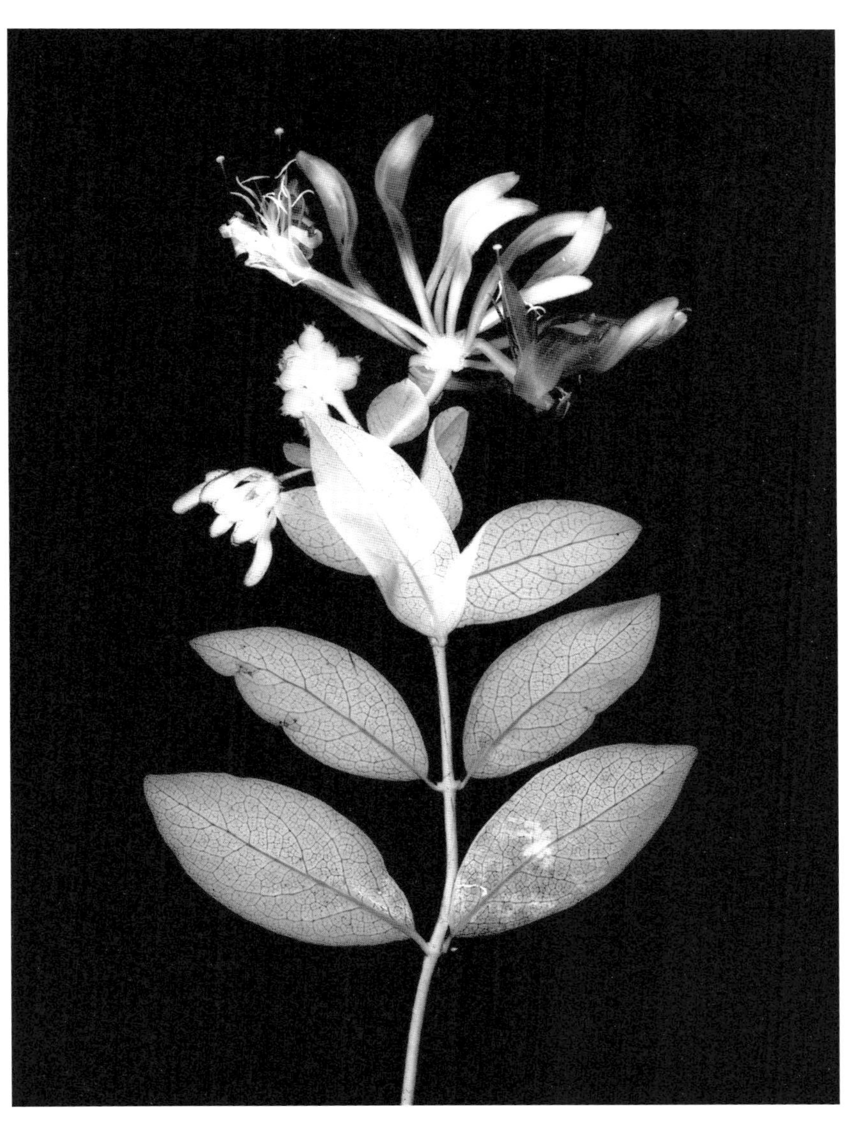

Honeysuckle
Lonicera periclymenum

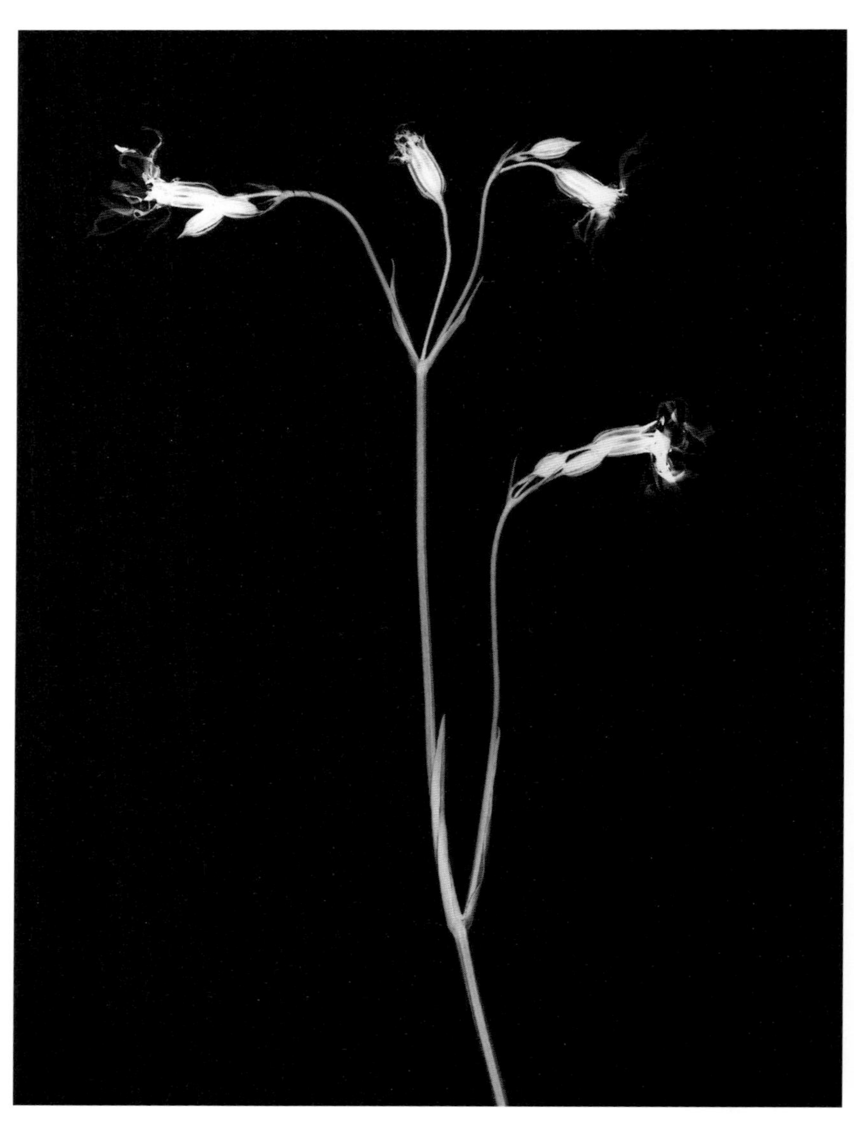

Ragged Robin
Lychnis flos-cuculi

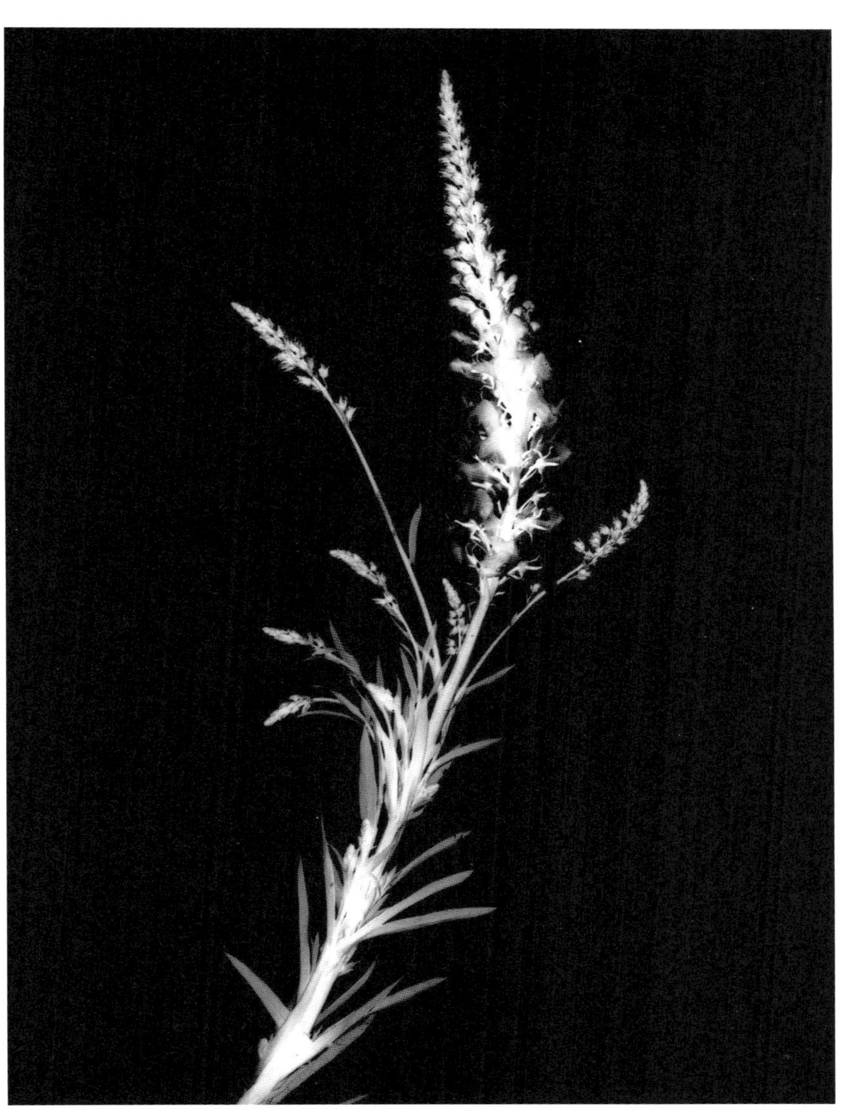

Purple Loosestrife
Lythrum salicaria

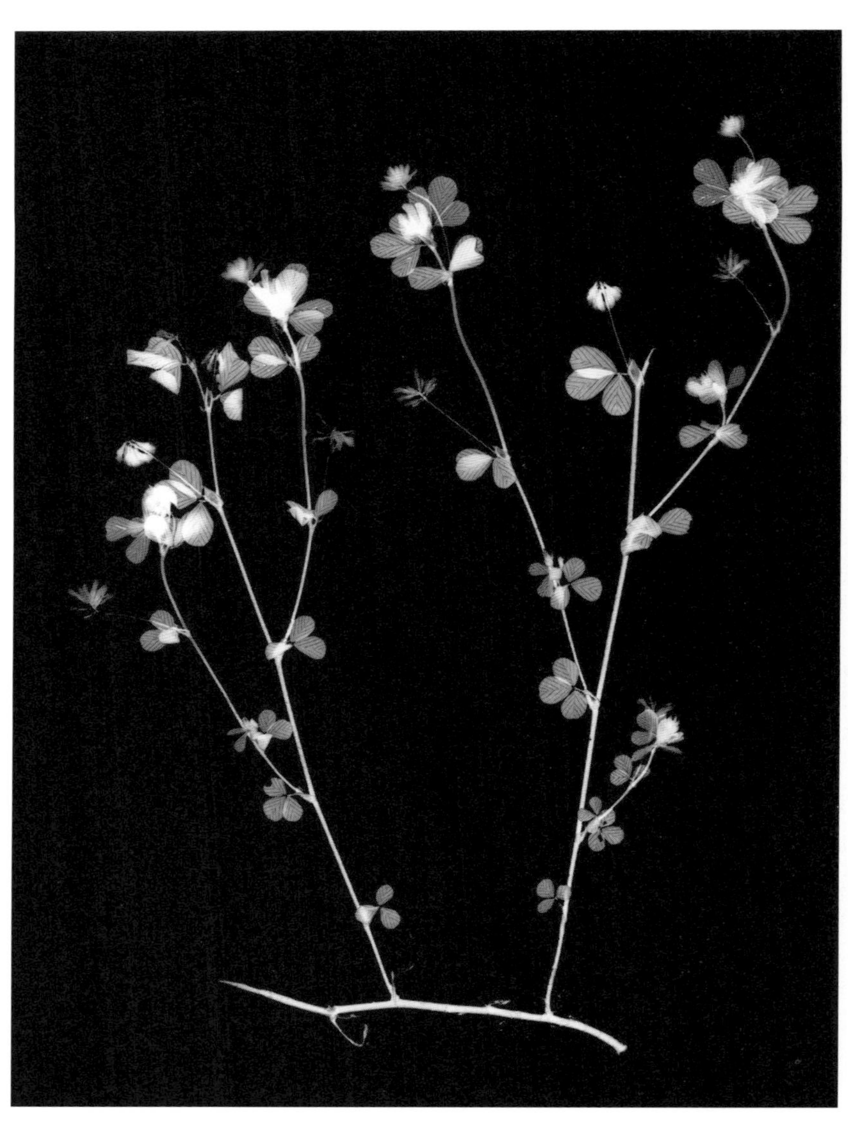

Black Medick
Medicago lupulina

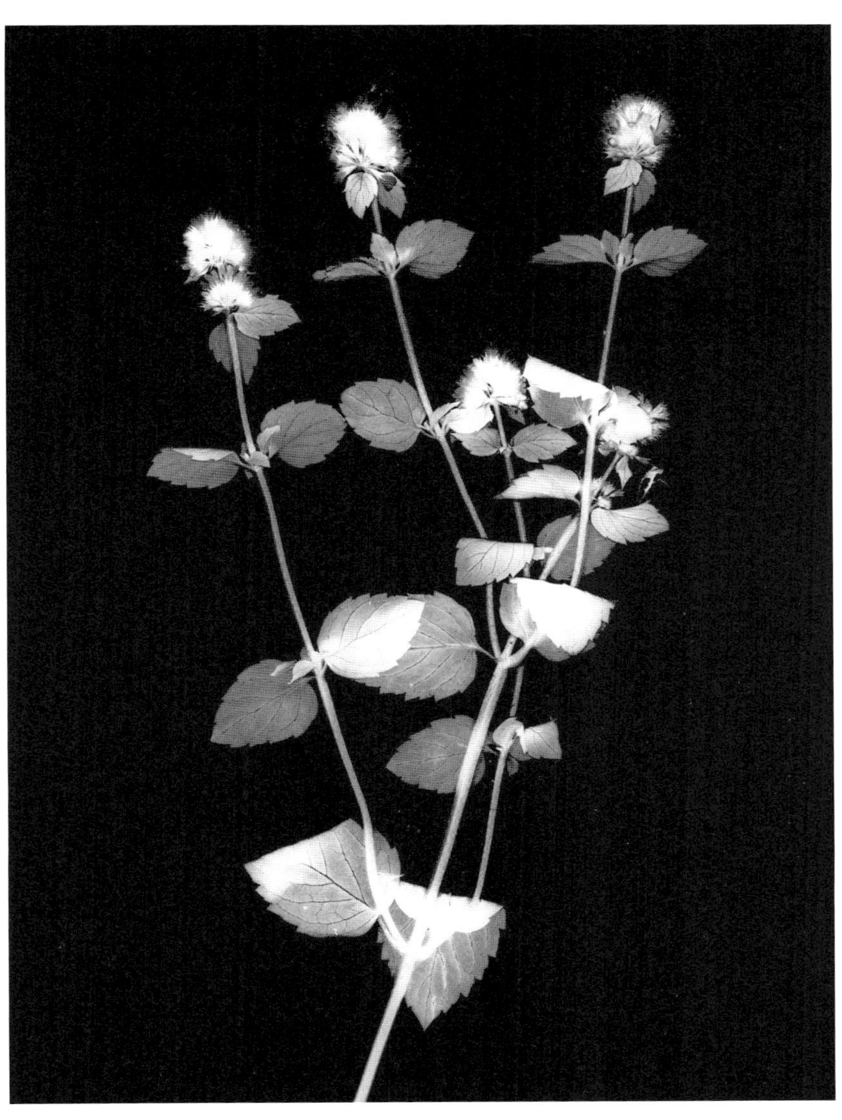

Water Mint
Mentha aquatica

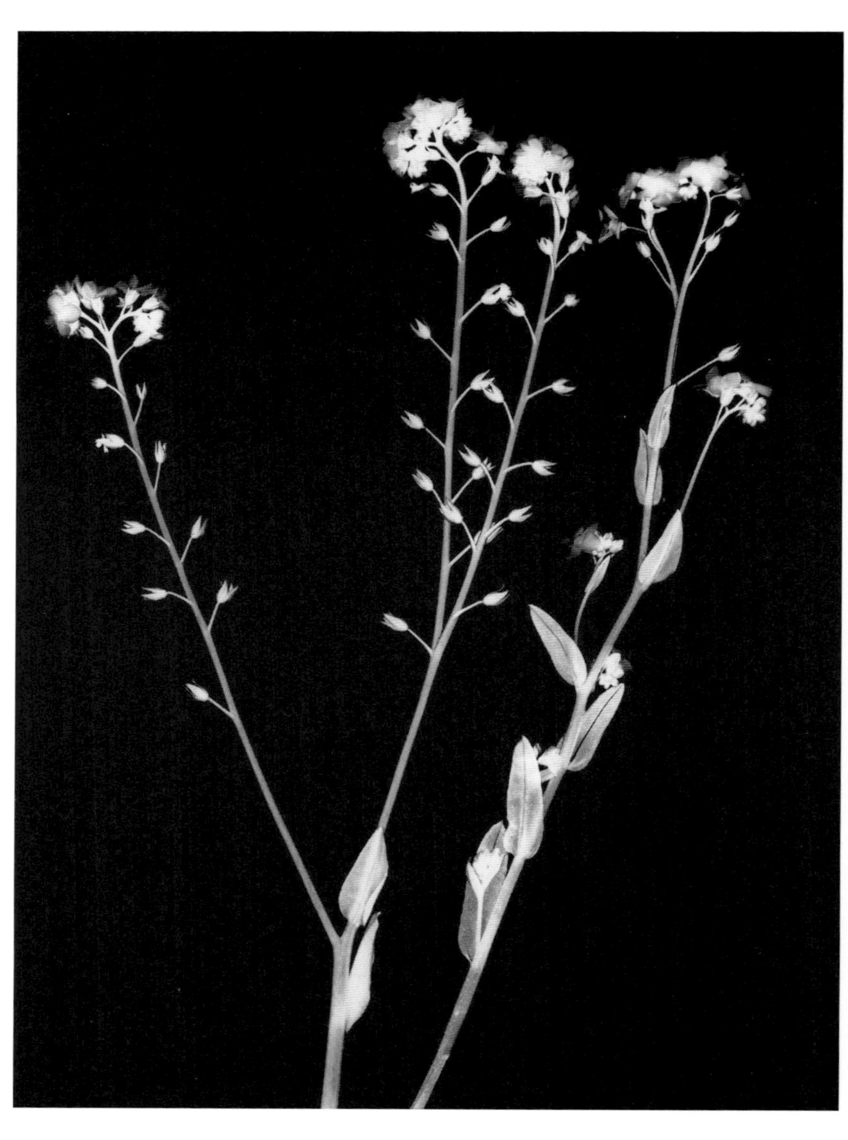

Forget-me-not
Myosotis sylvatica

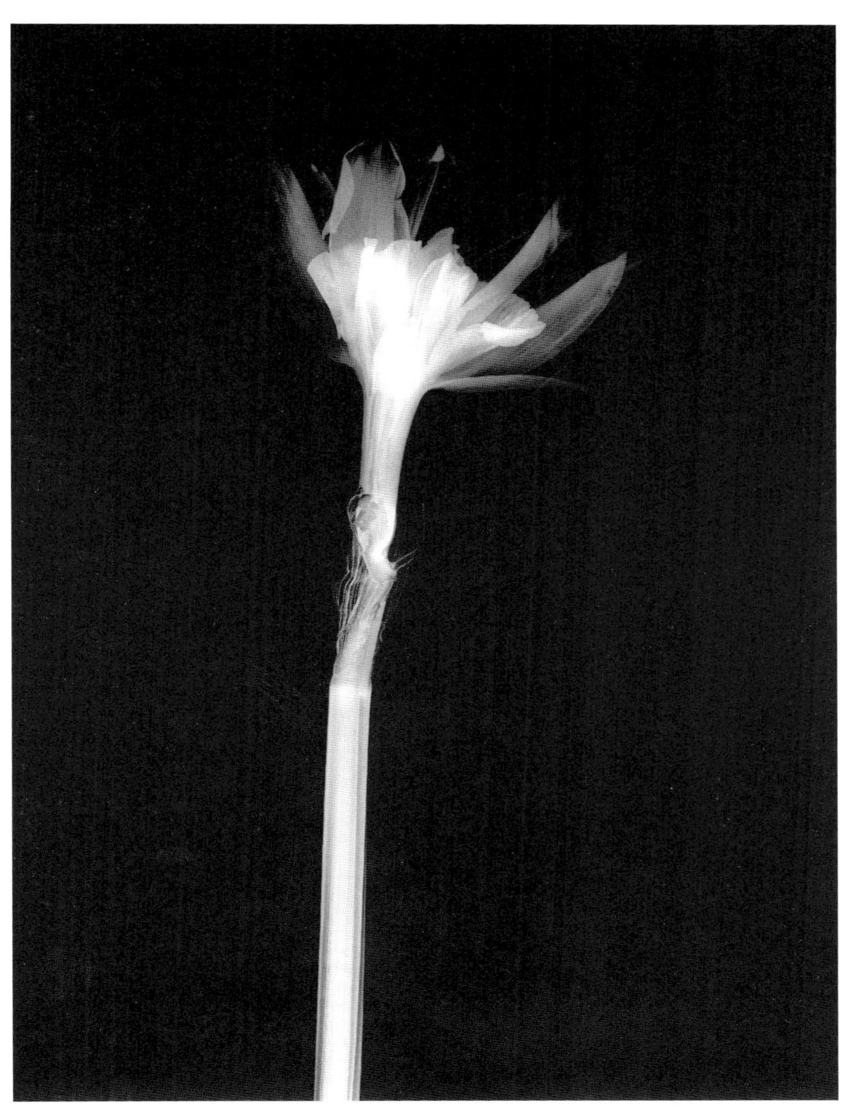

Daffodil
Narcissus

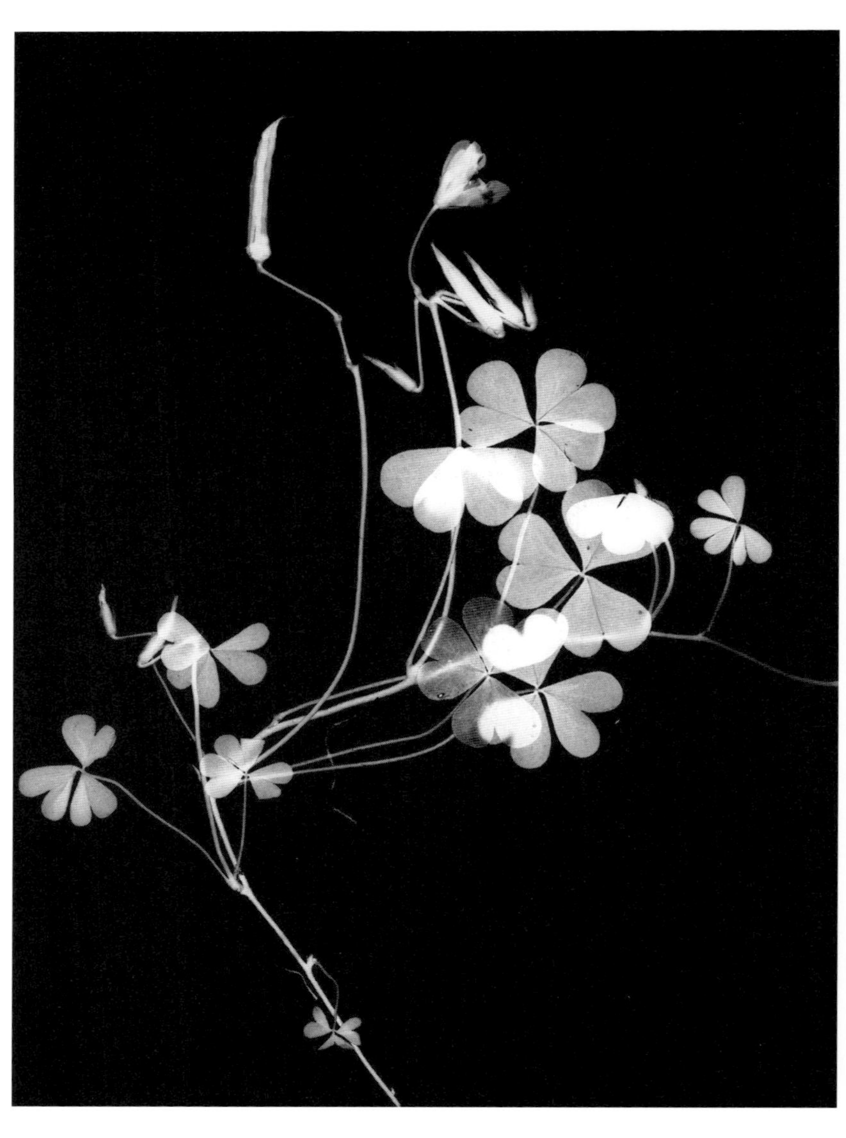

Yellow Wood Sorrel
Oxalis stricta

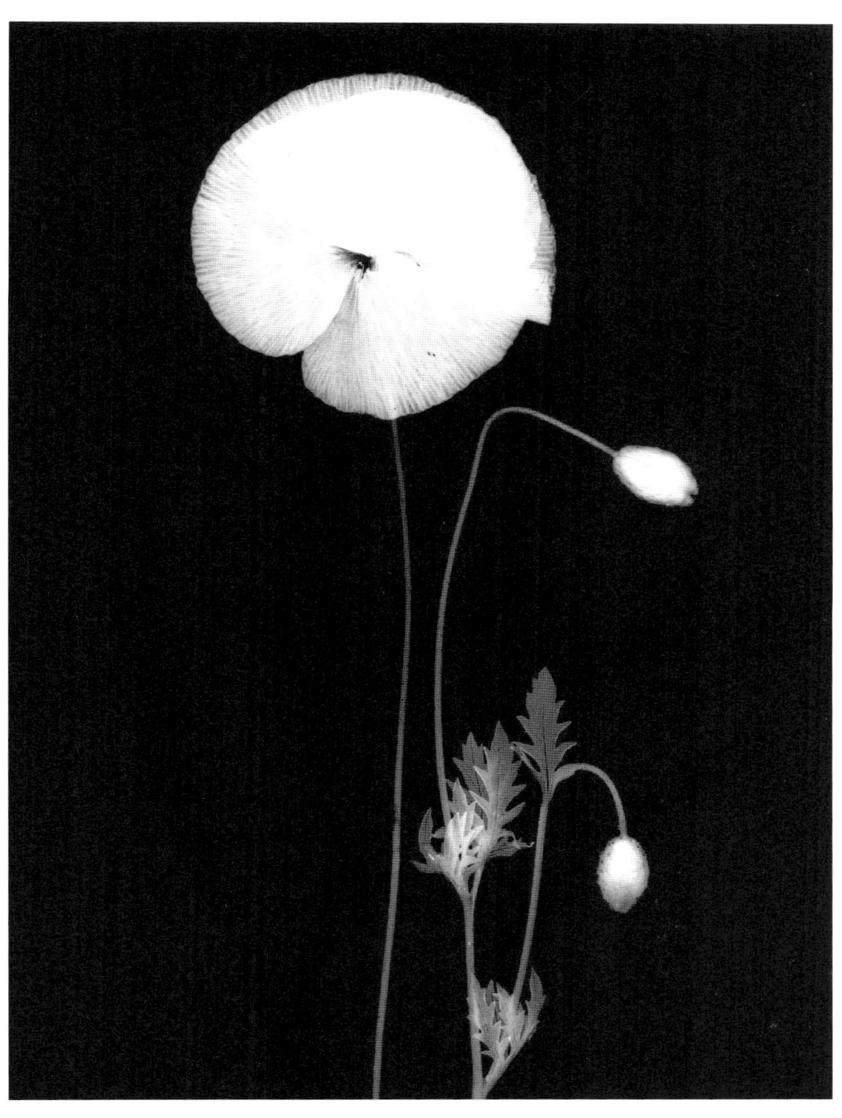

Flanders Poppy
Papaver rhoeas

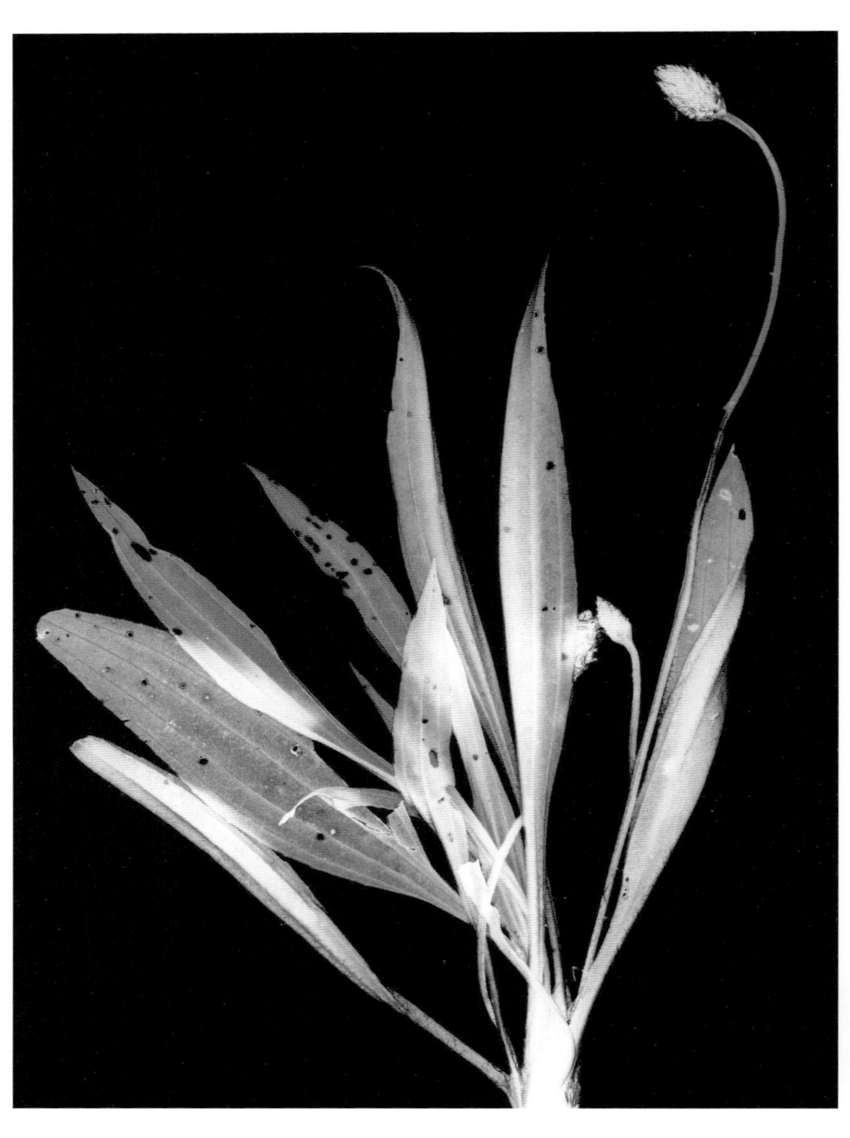

Ribwort Plantain
Plantago lanceolata

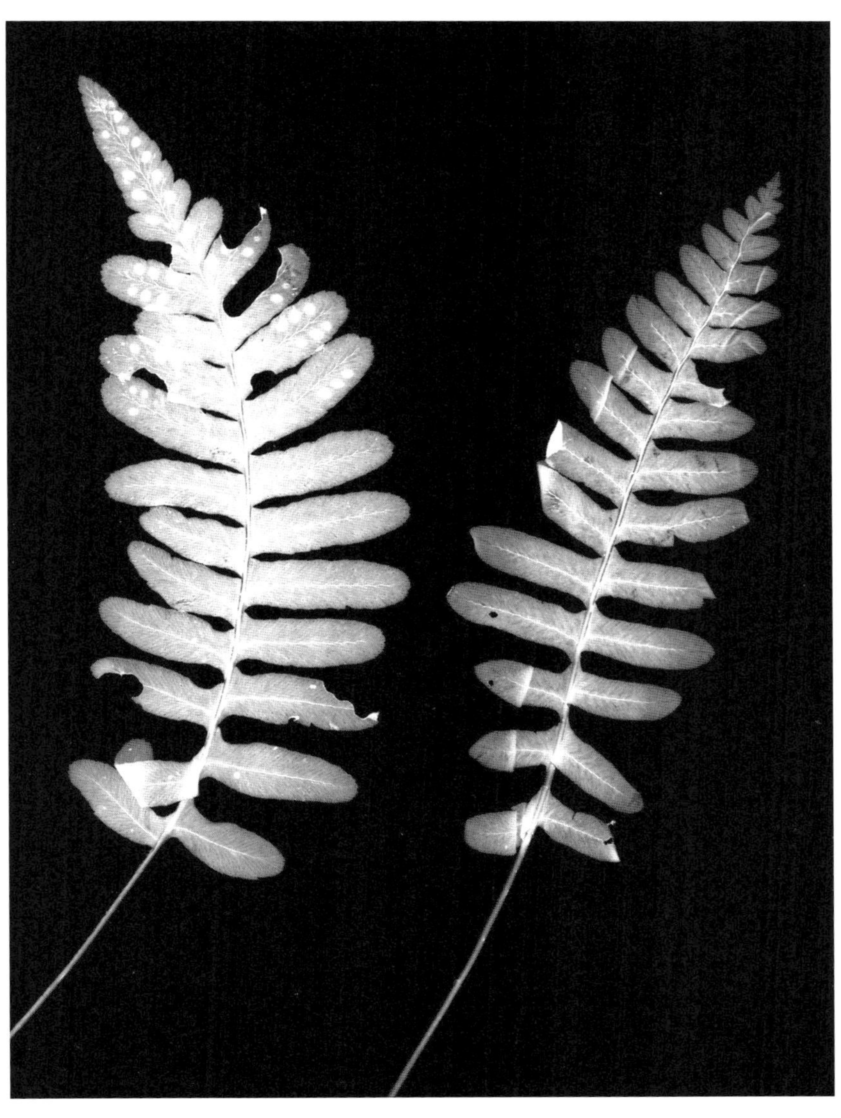

Common Polypody
Polypodium vulgare

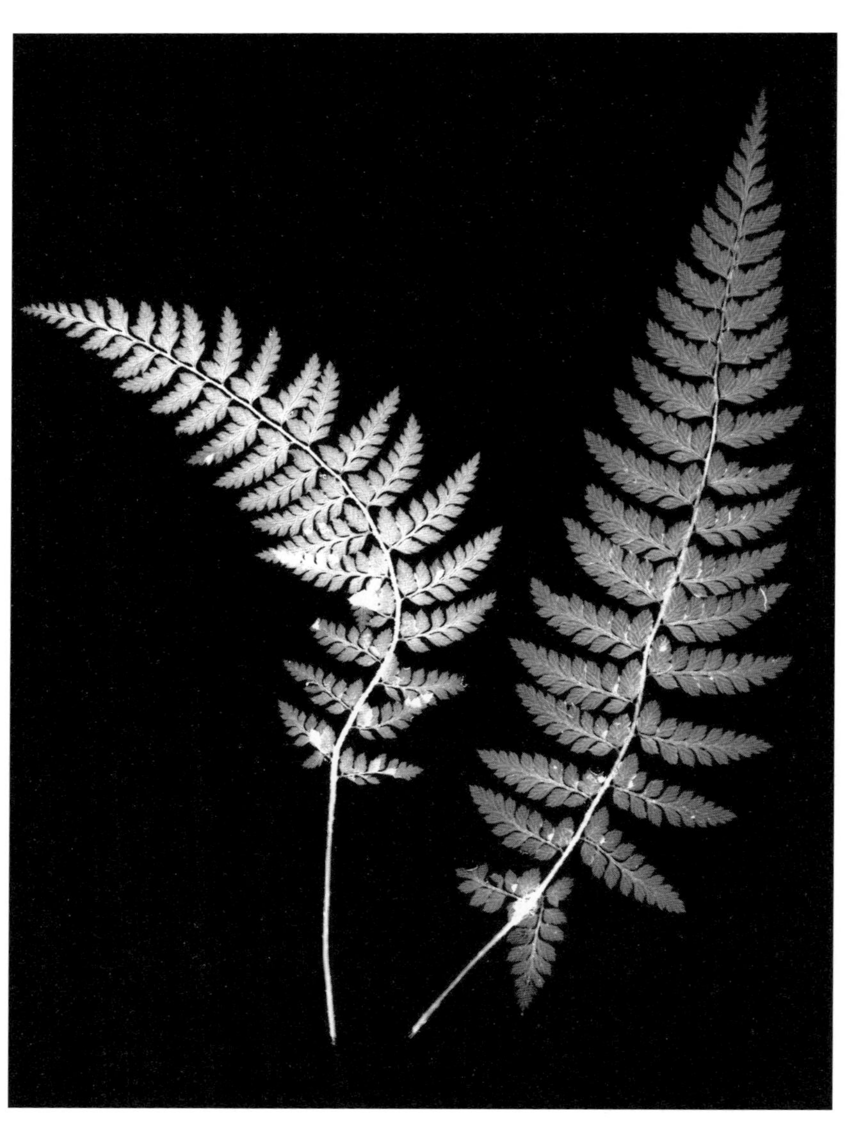

Soft Shield Fern
Polystichum setiferum

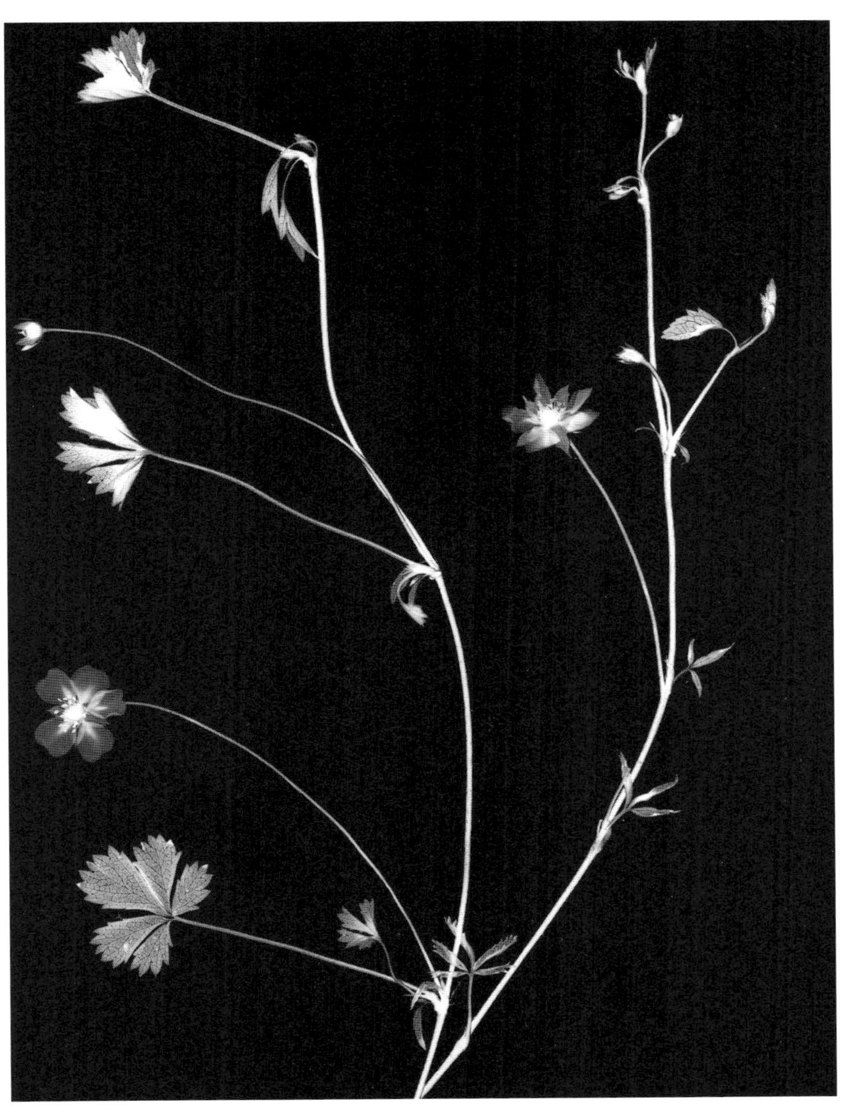

Creeping Cinquefoil
Potentilla reptans

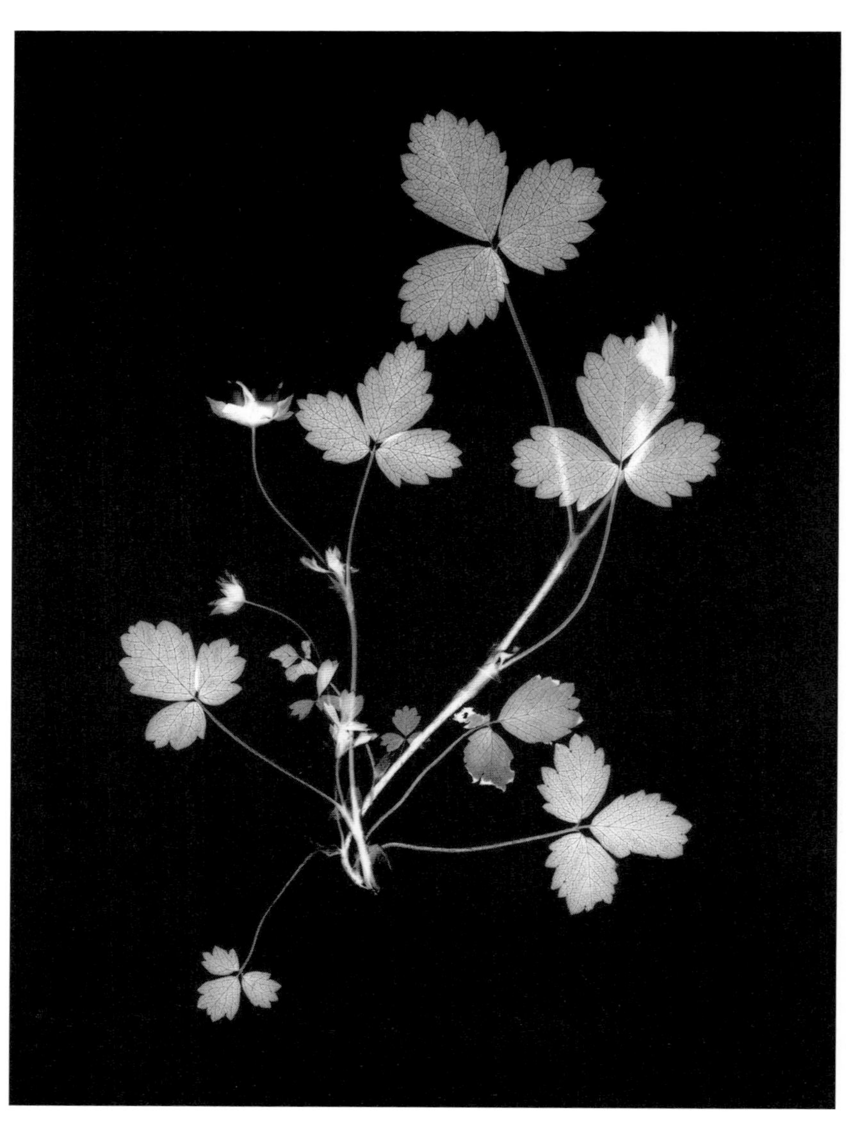

Barren Strawberry
Potentilla sterilis

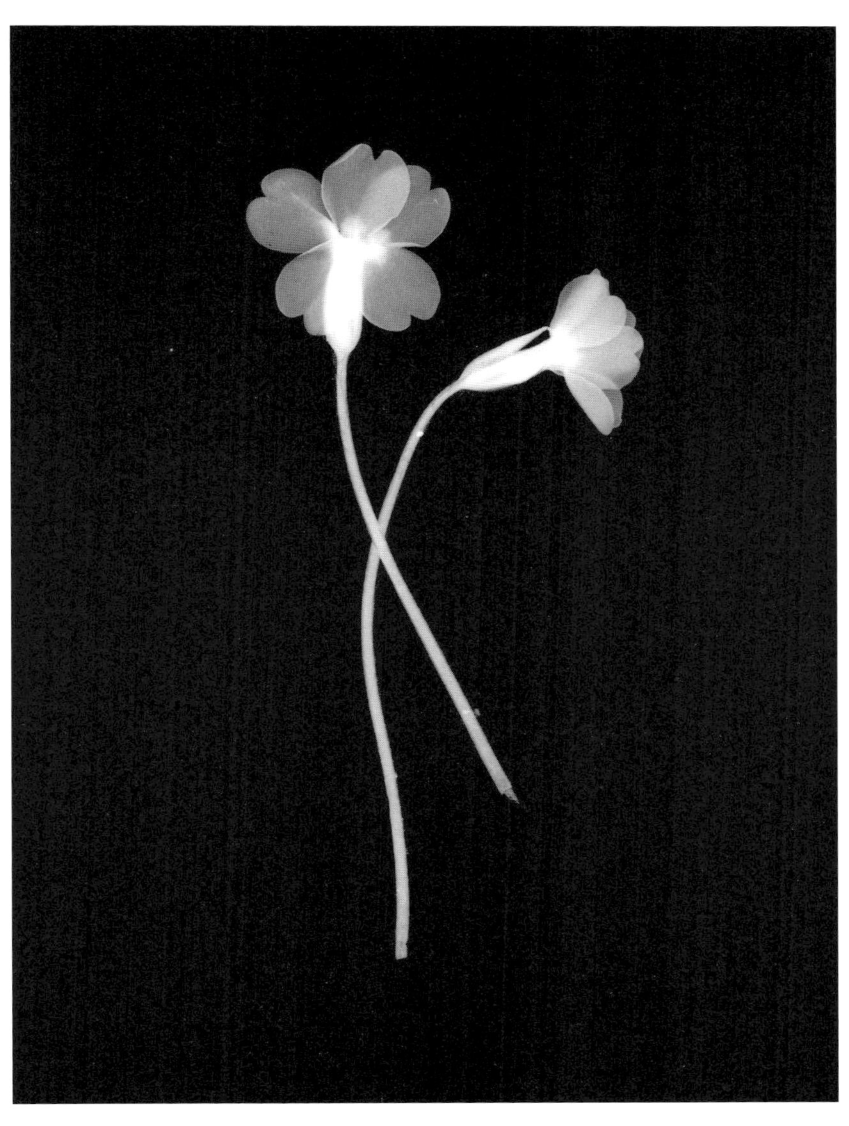

Primrose
Primula vulgaris

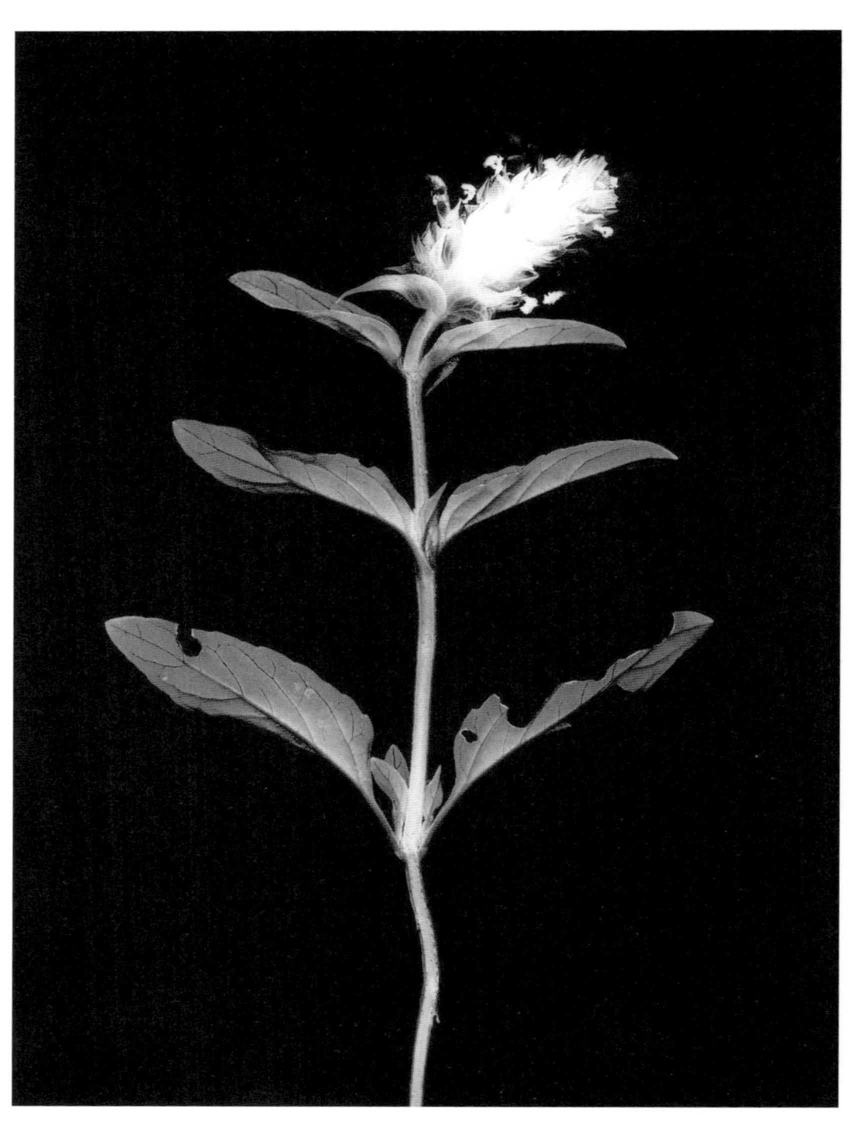

Self-heal

Prunella vulgaris

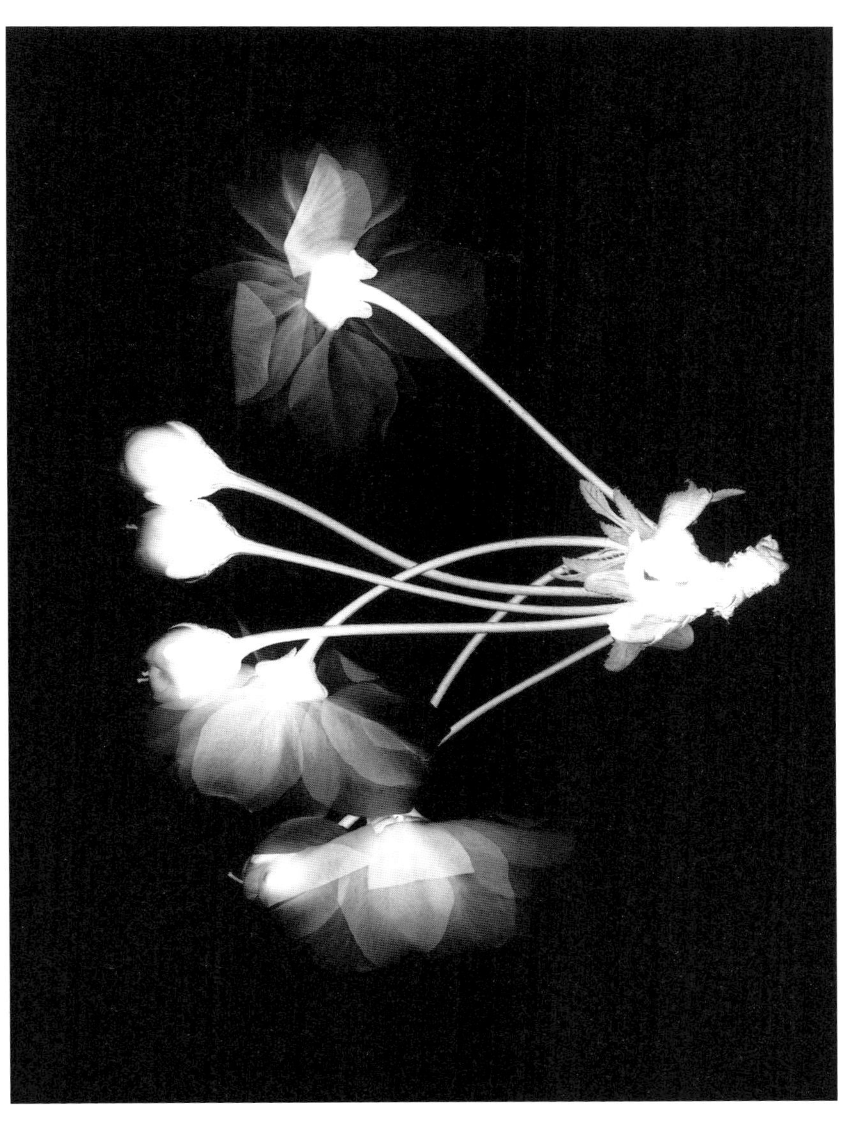

Wild Cherry
Prunus avium

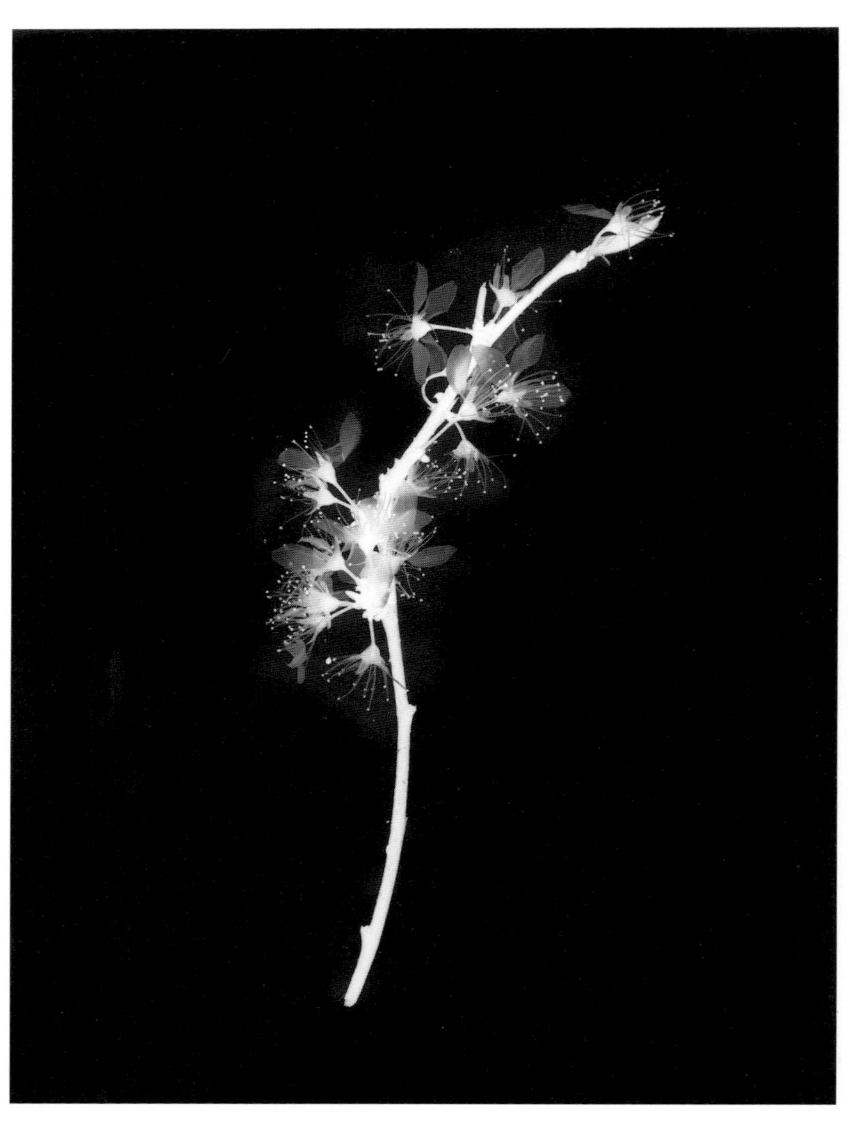

Sloe
Prunus spinosa

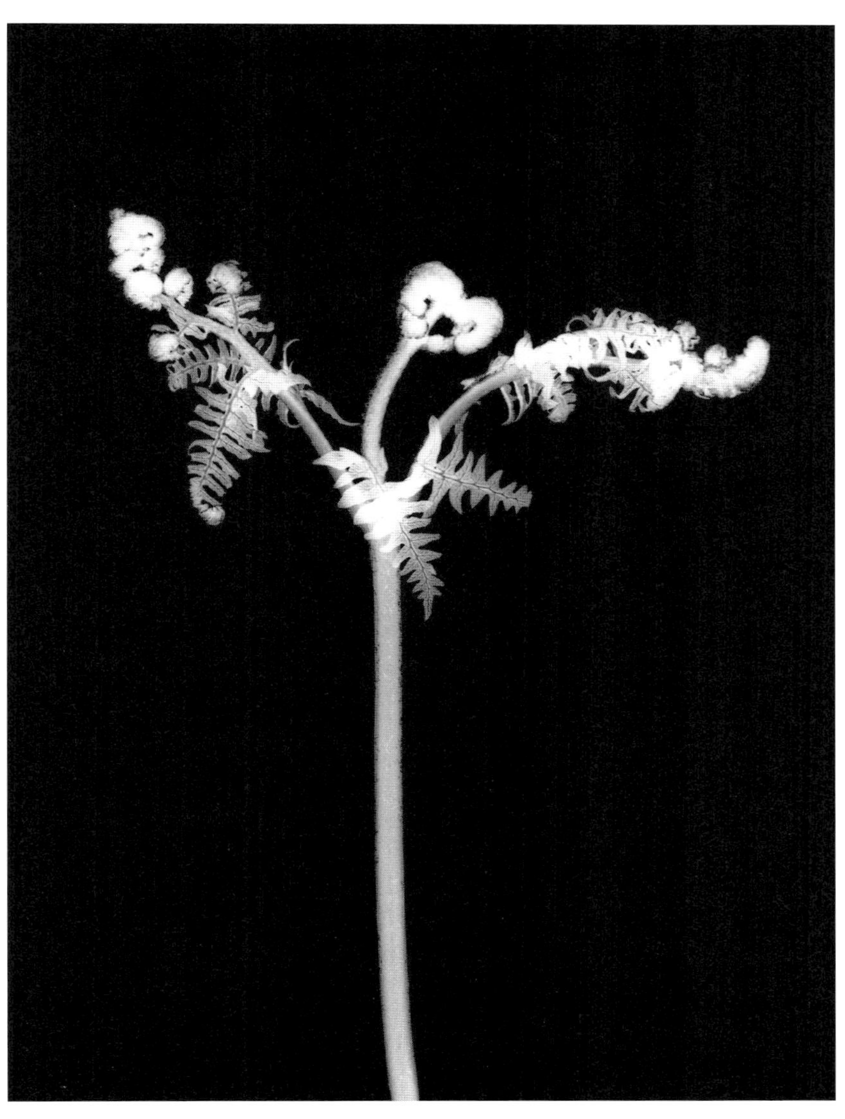

Bracken
Pteridium aquilinum

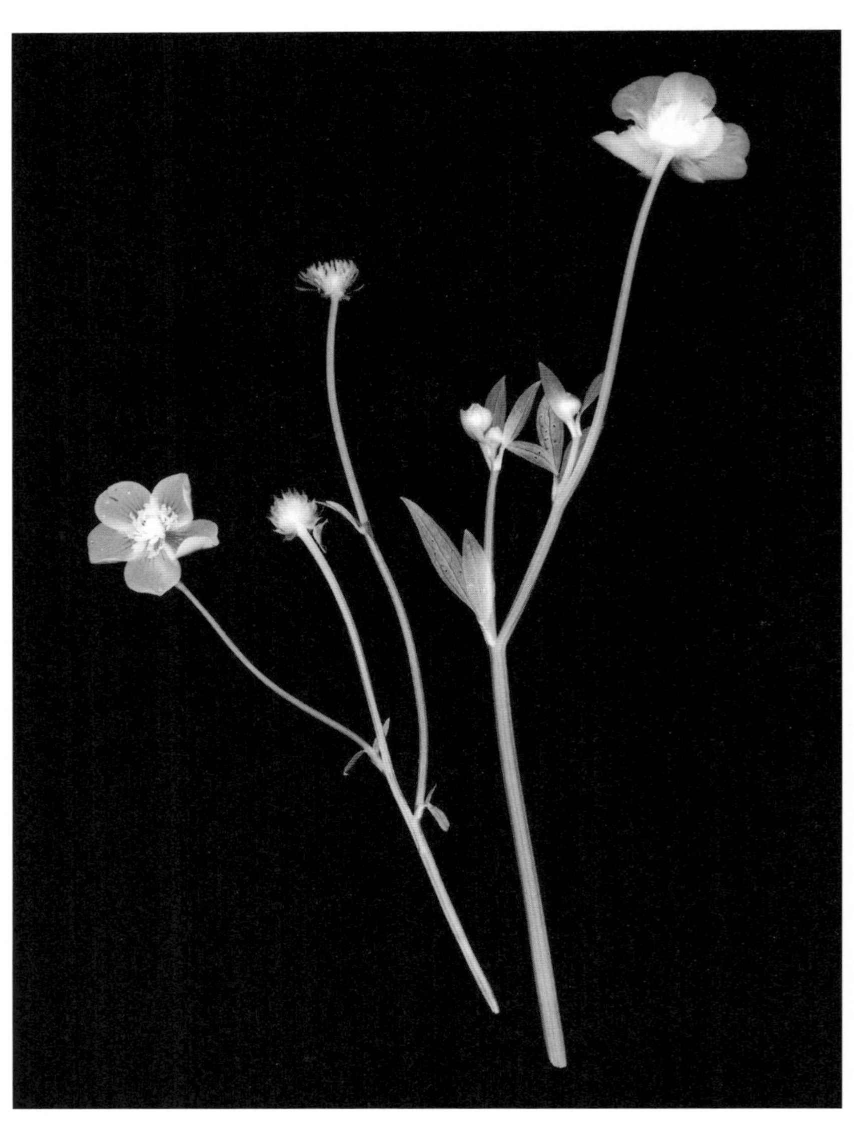

Creeping Buttercup
Ranunculus repens

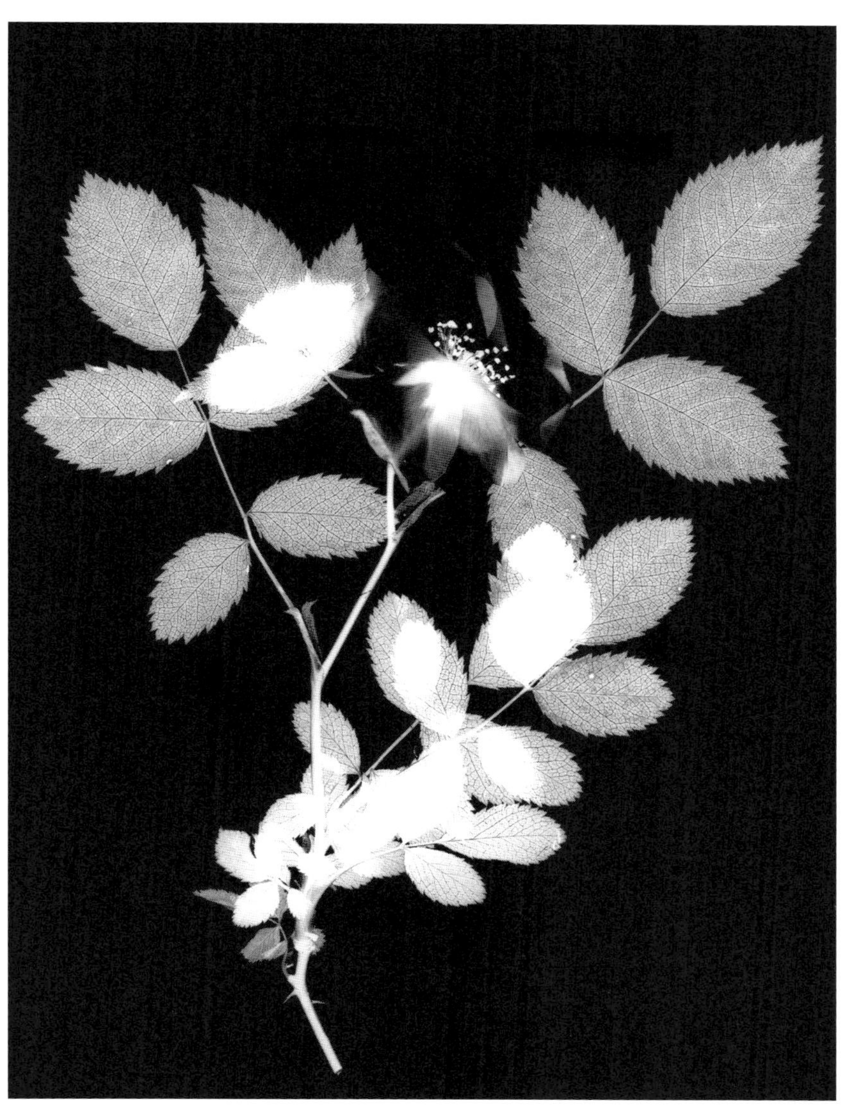

Dog Rose

Rosa canina

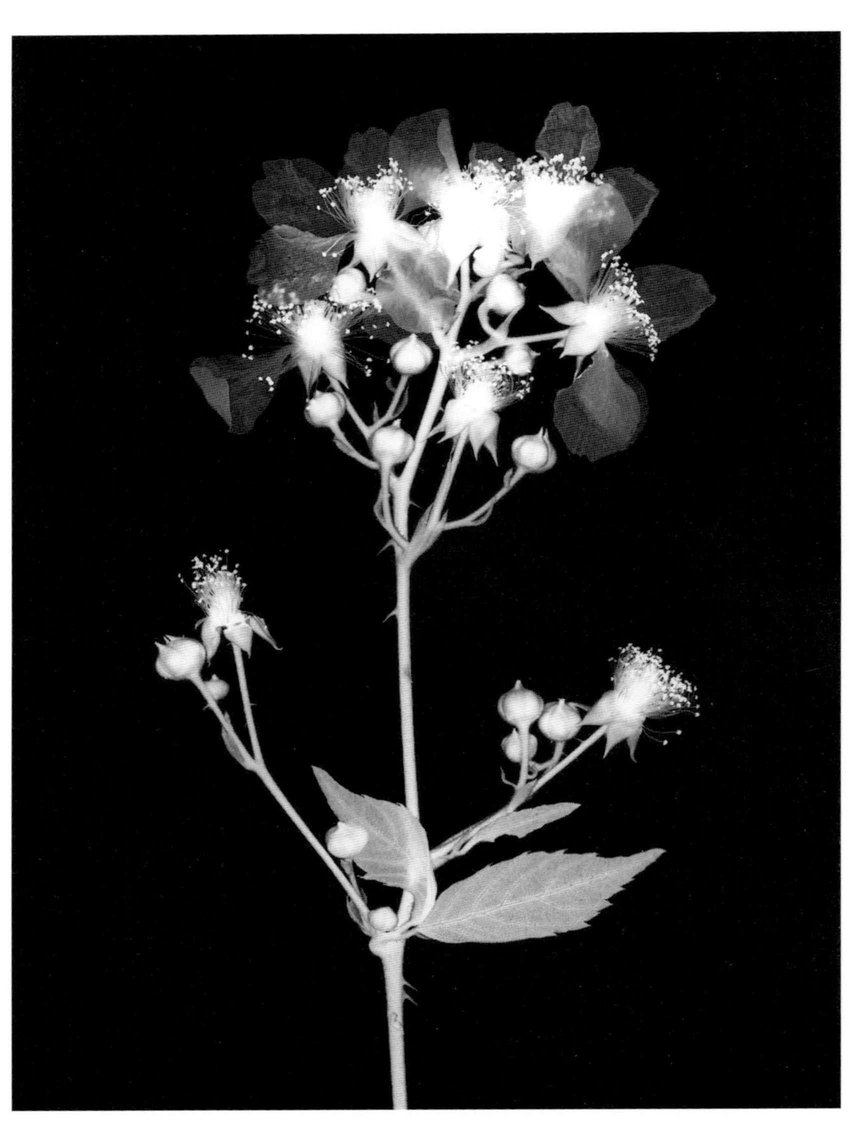

Blackberry Bramble
Rubus fructicosus

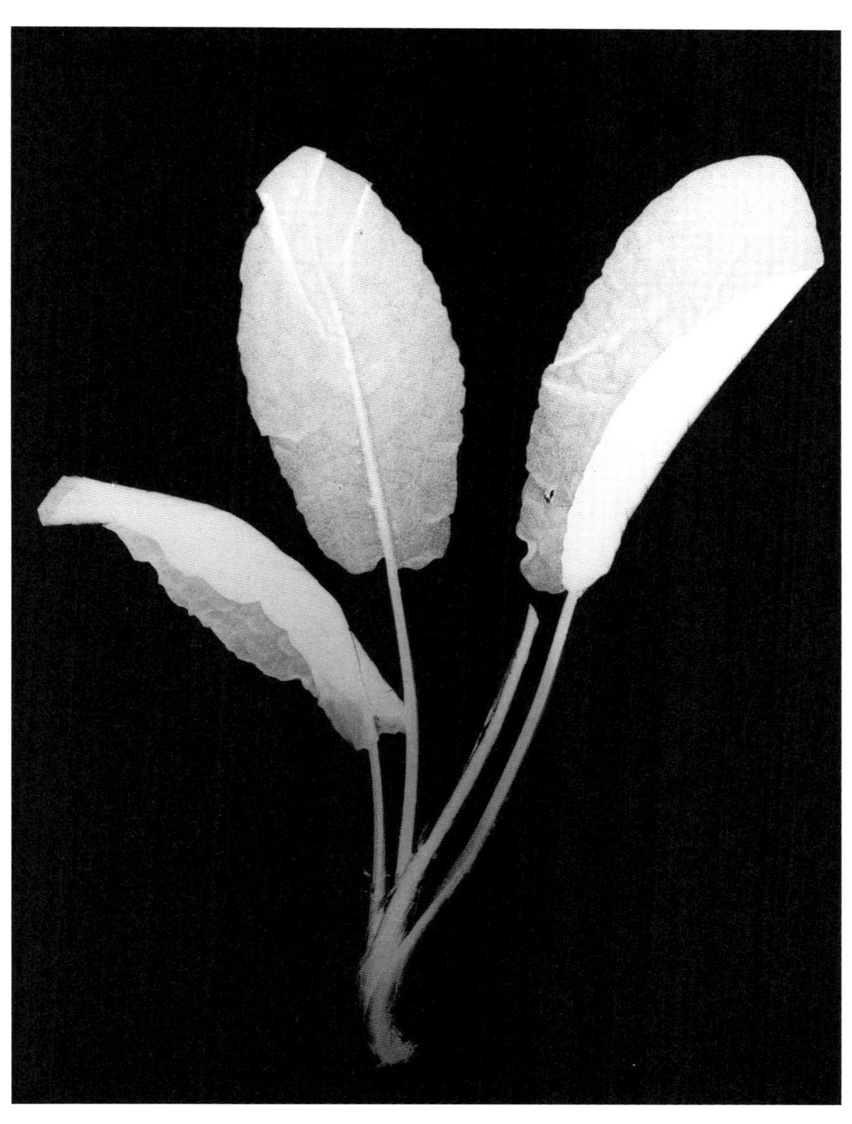

Broad-leaved Dock
Rumex obtusifolius

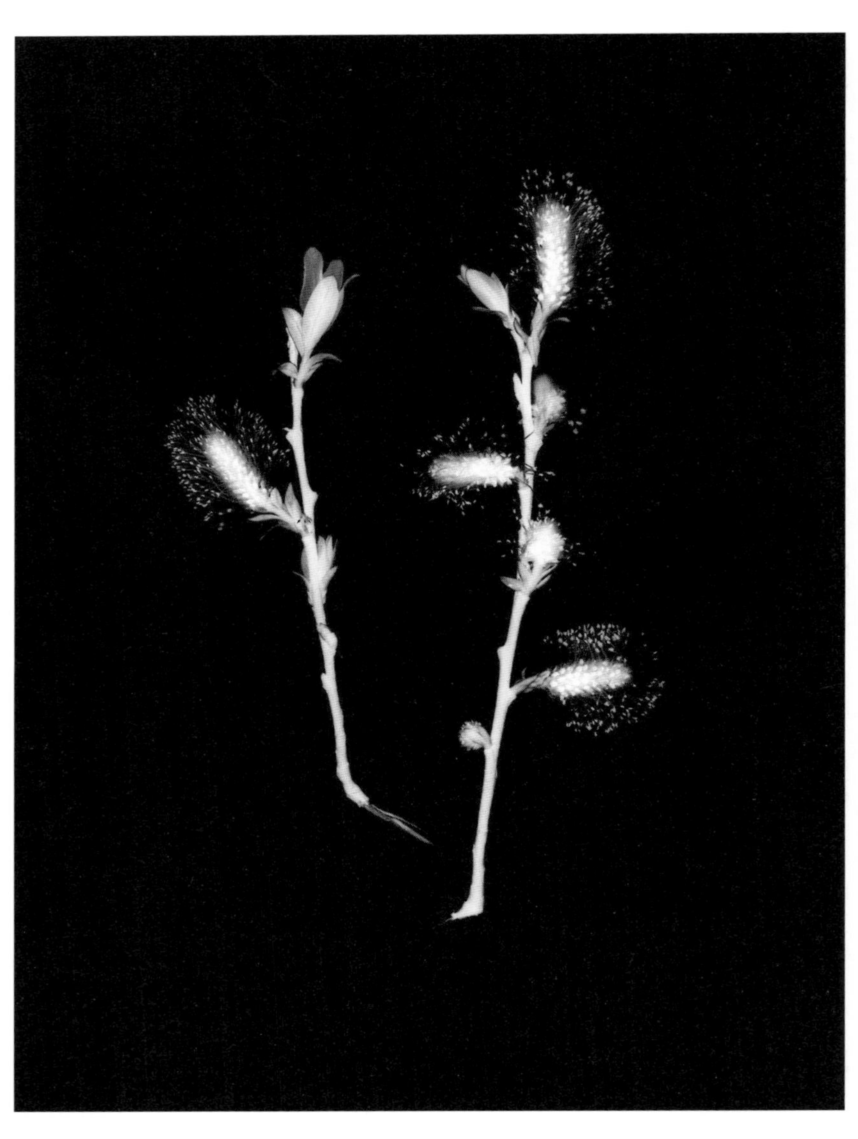

Grey Willow
Salix cinerea

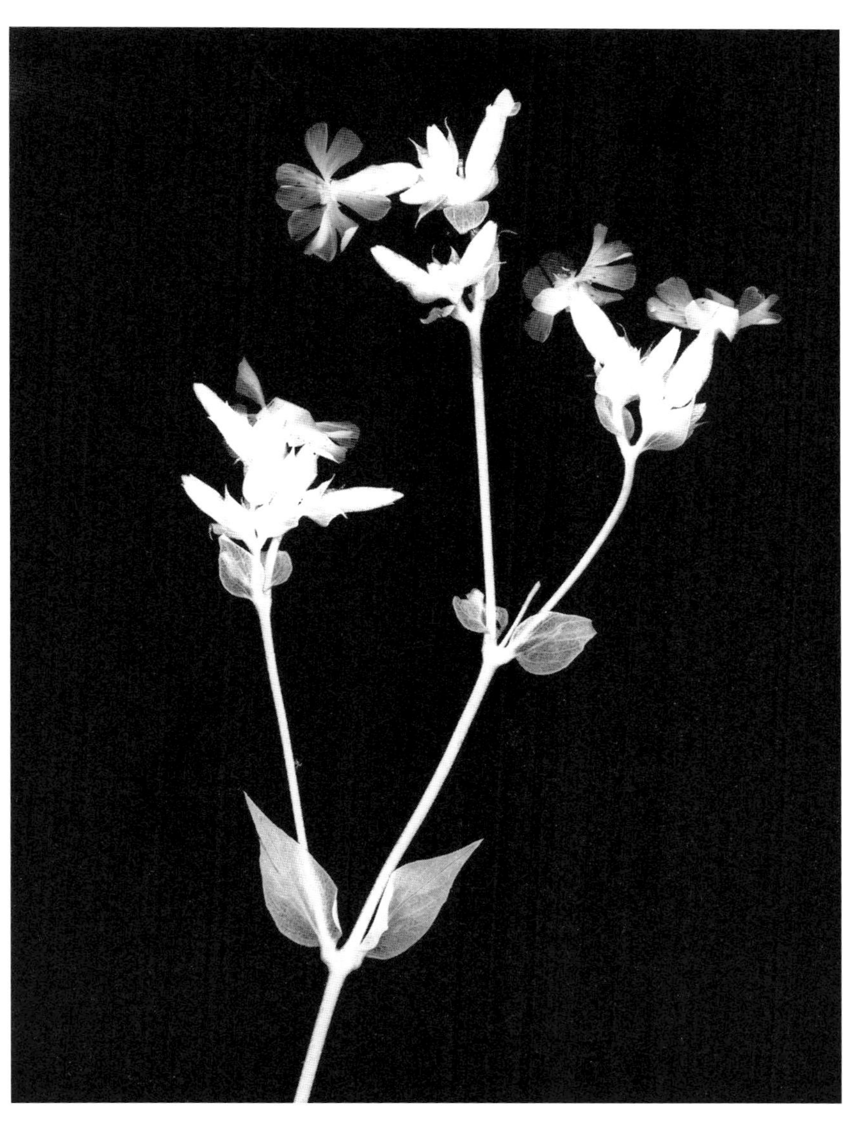

Red Campion
Silene dioica

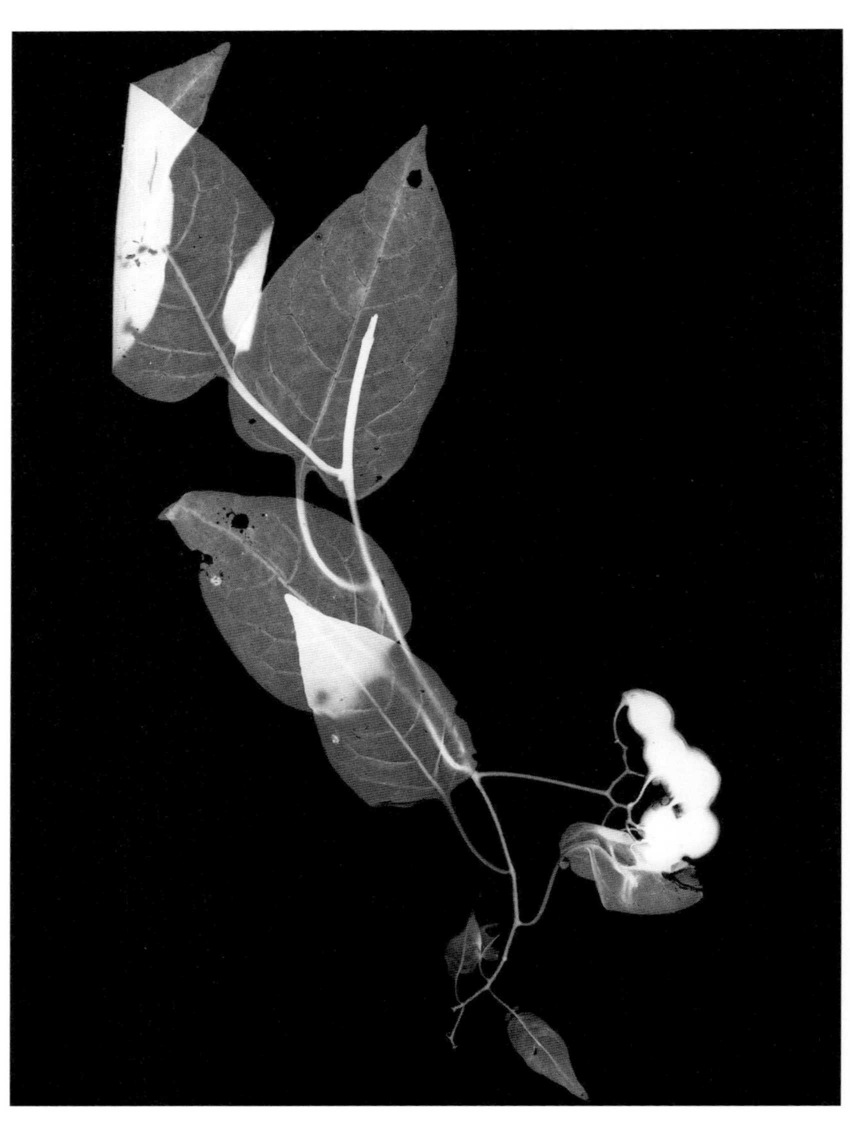

Bittersweet Nightshade
Solanum dulcamara

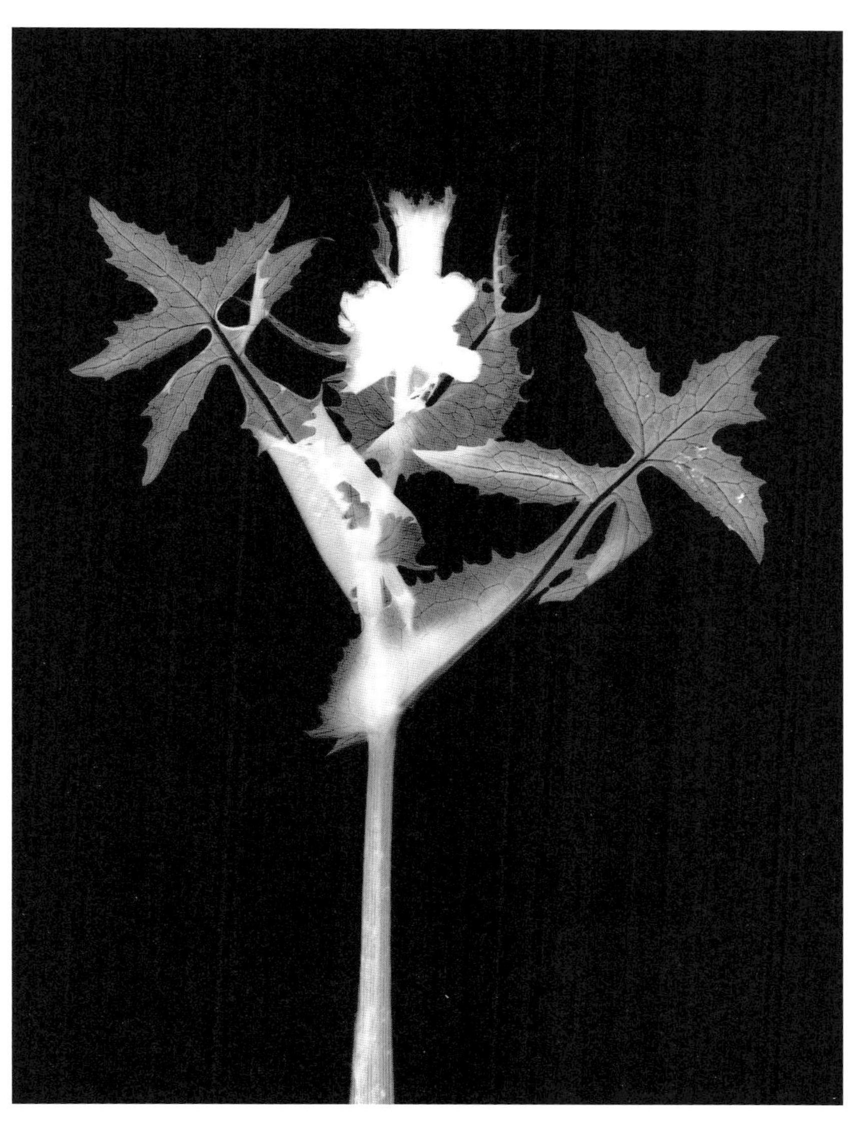

Common Sowthistle
Sonchus oleraceus

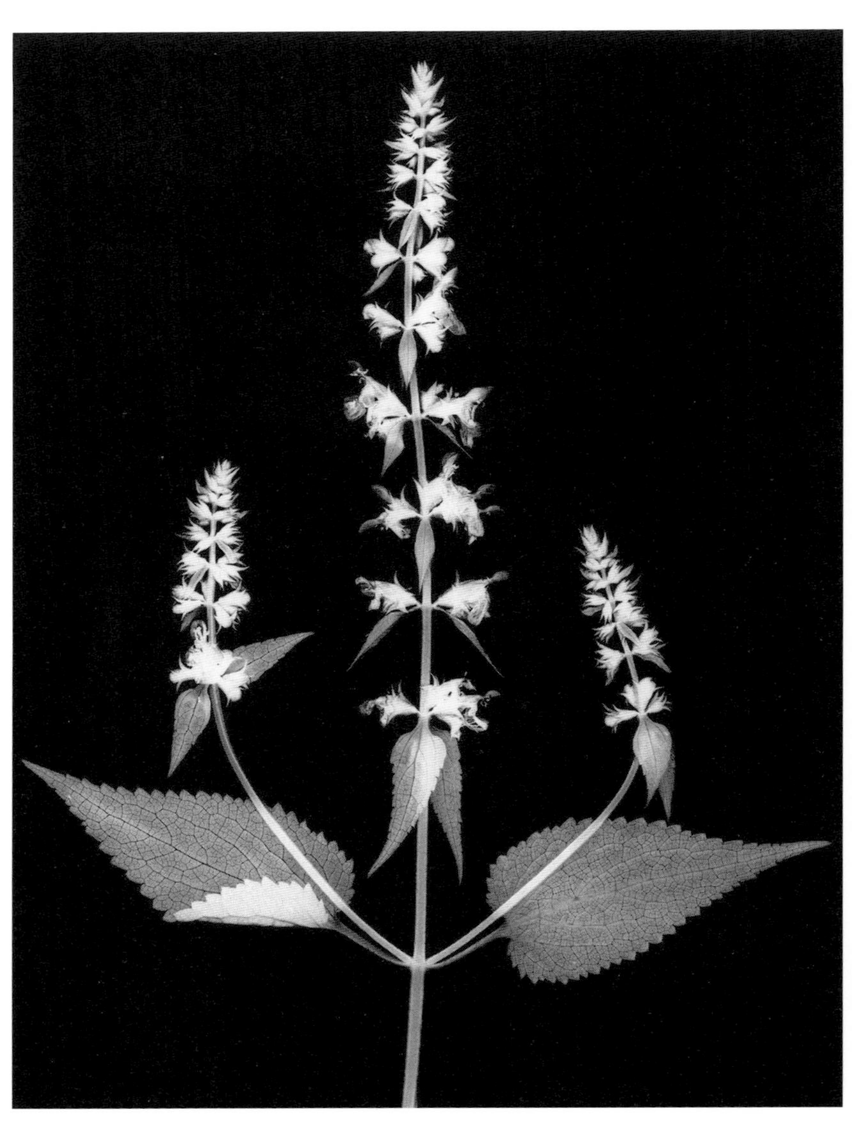

Hedge Woundwort
Stachys sylvatica

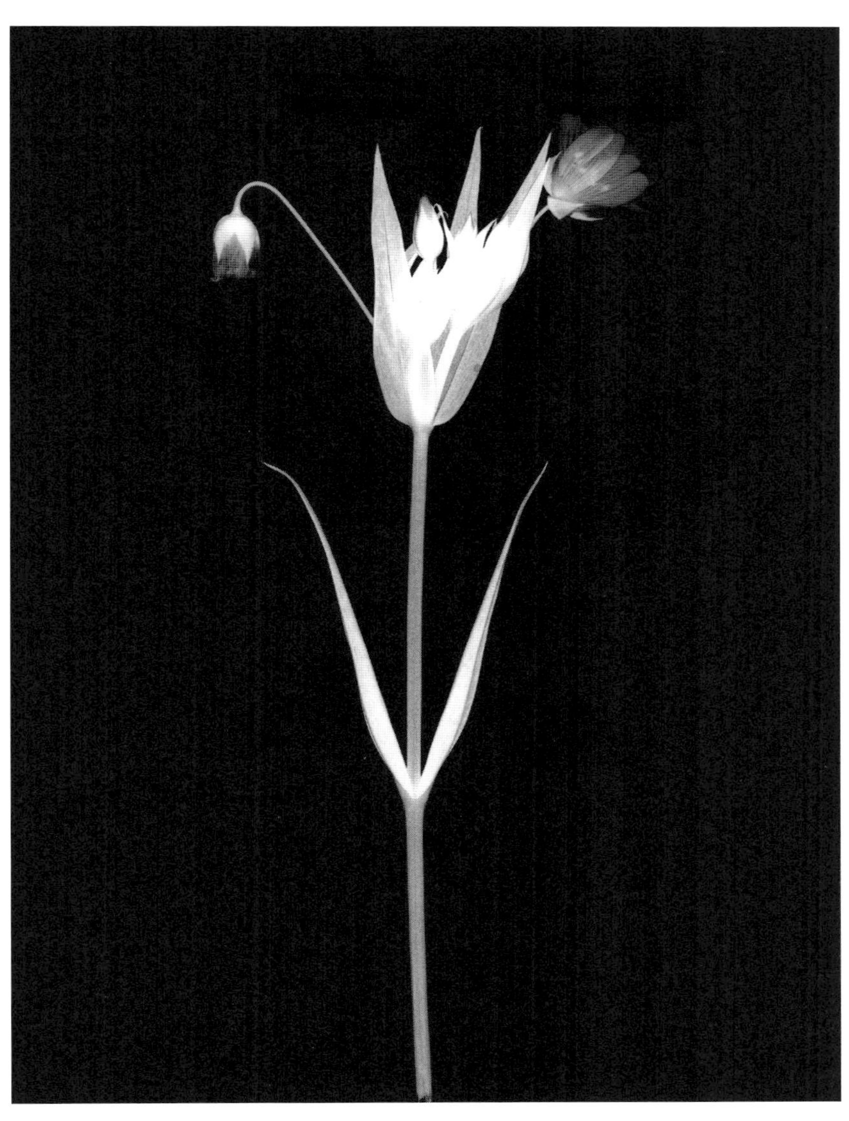

Greater Stitchwort
Stellaria holostea

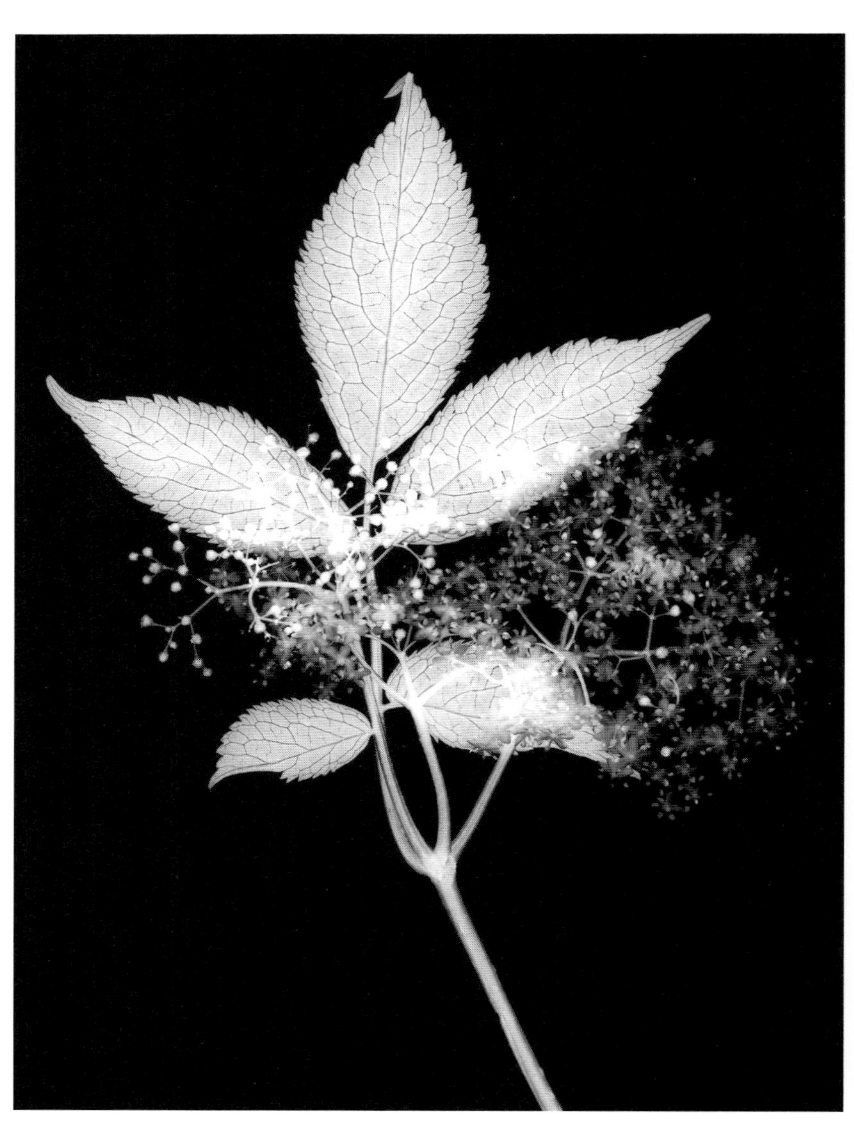

Elderflower
Sumbuscus nigra

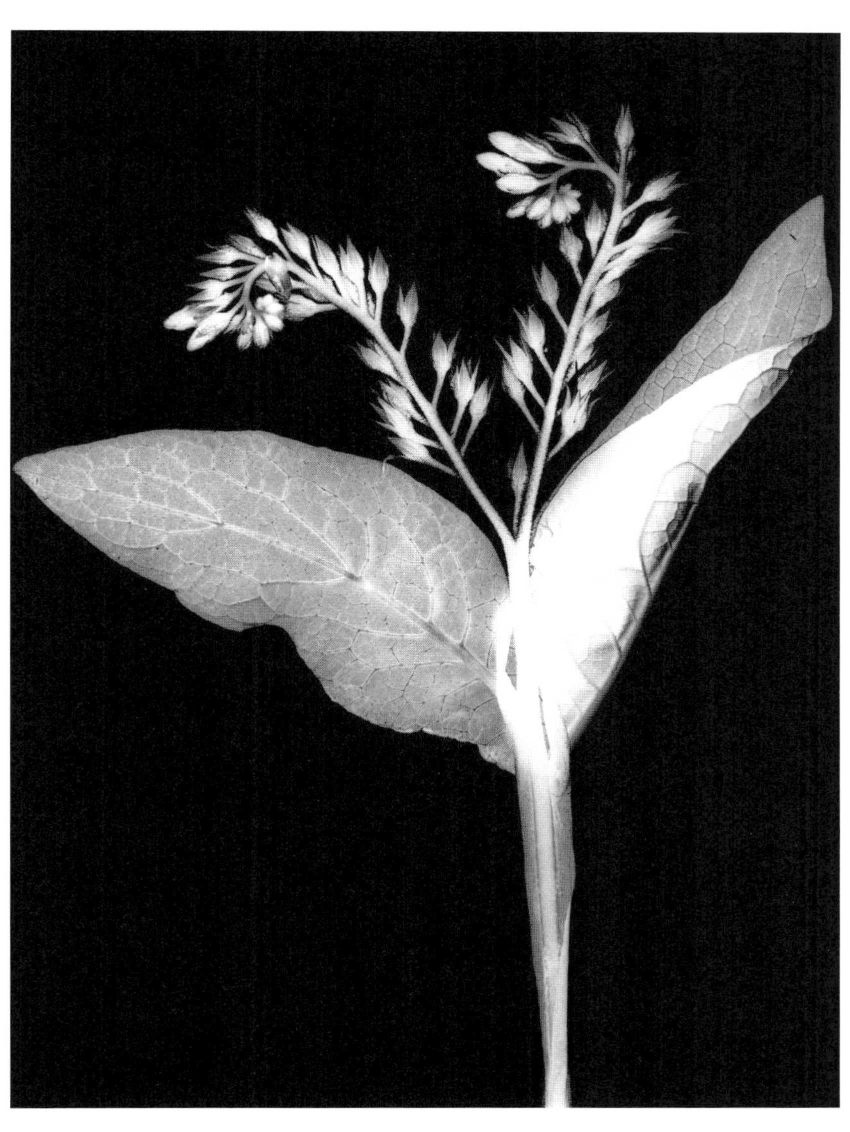

Comfrey
Symphytum officinale

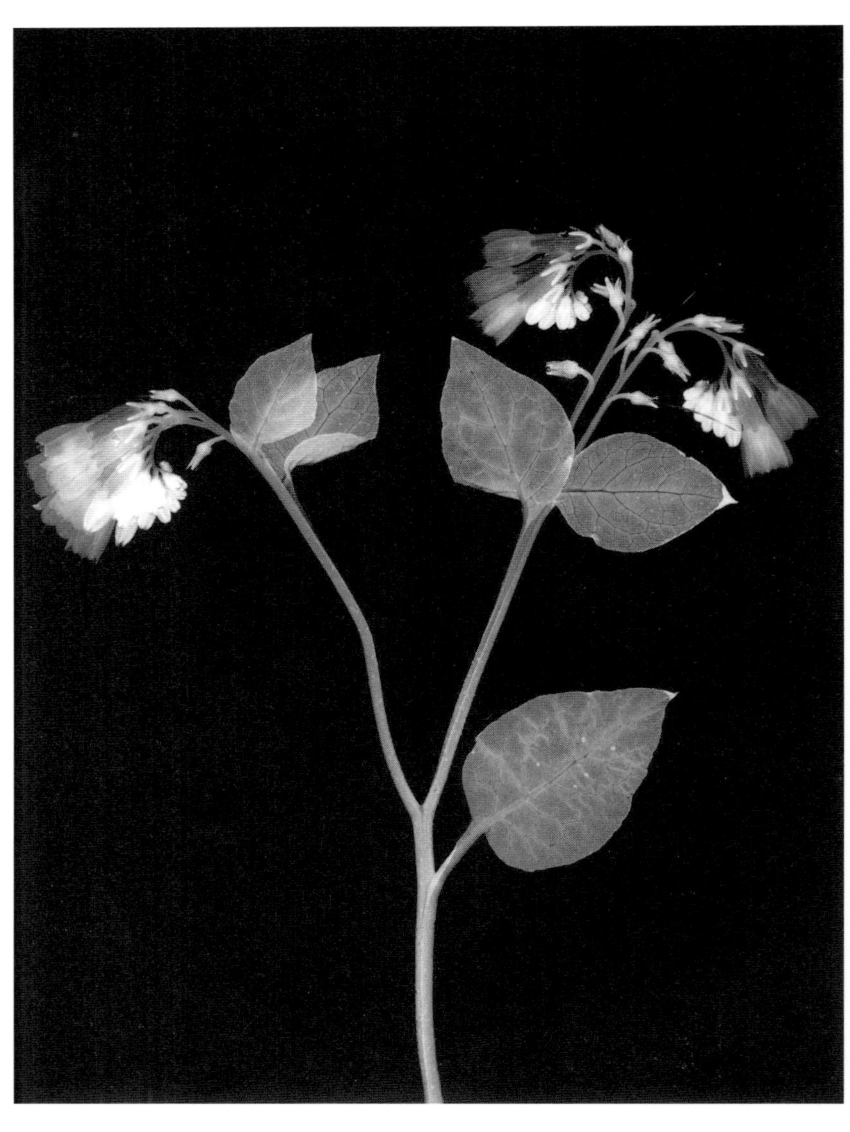

Tuberous Comfrey
Symphytum tuberosum

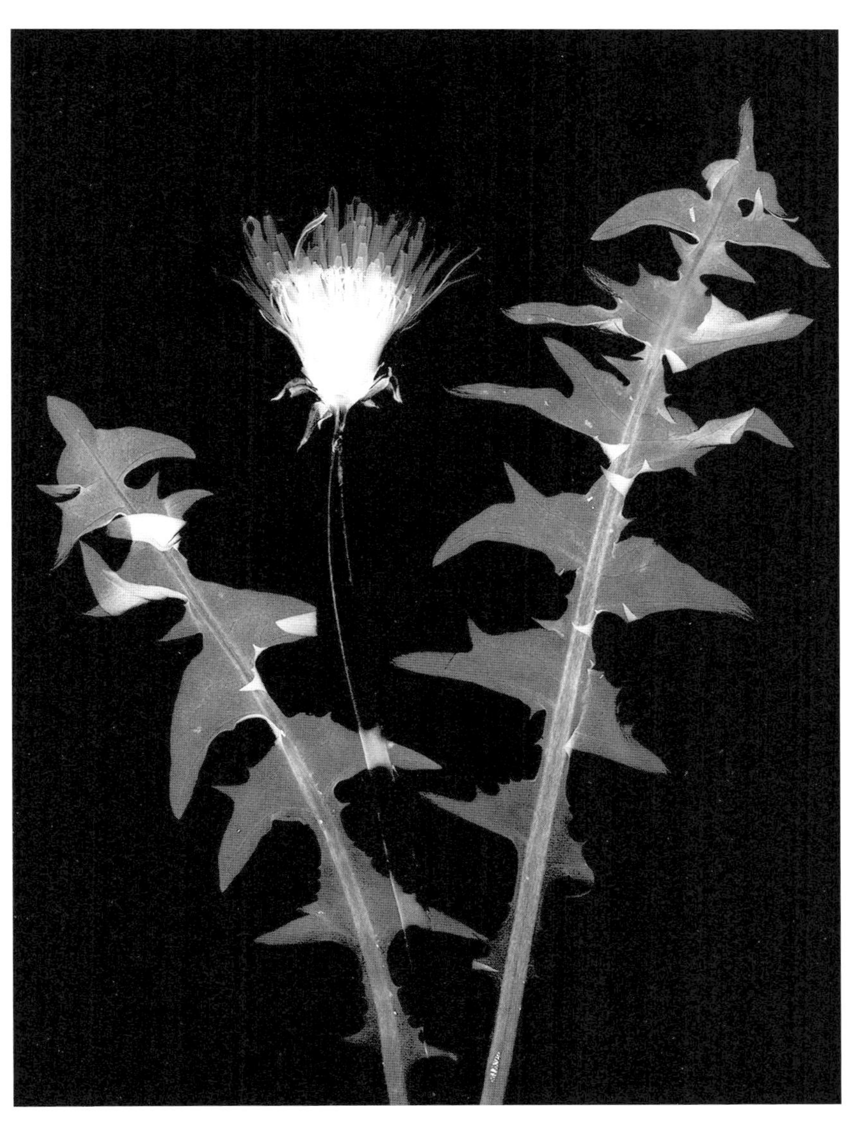

Dandelion
Taraxacum officinale

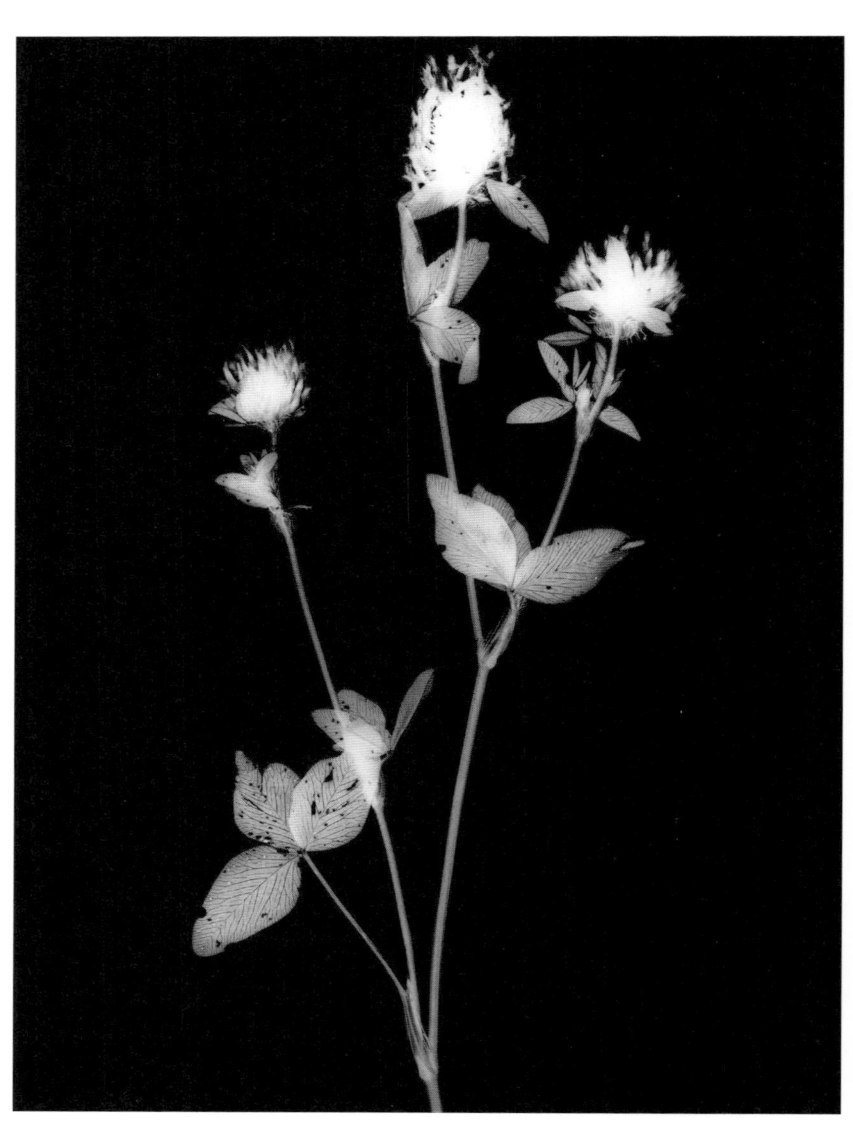

Red Clover
Trifolium pratense

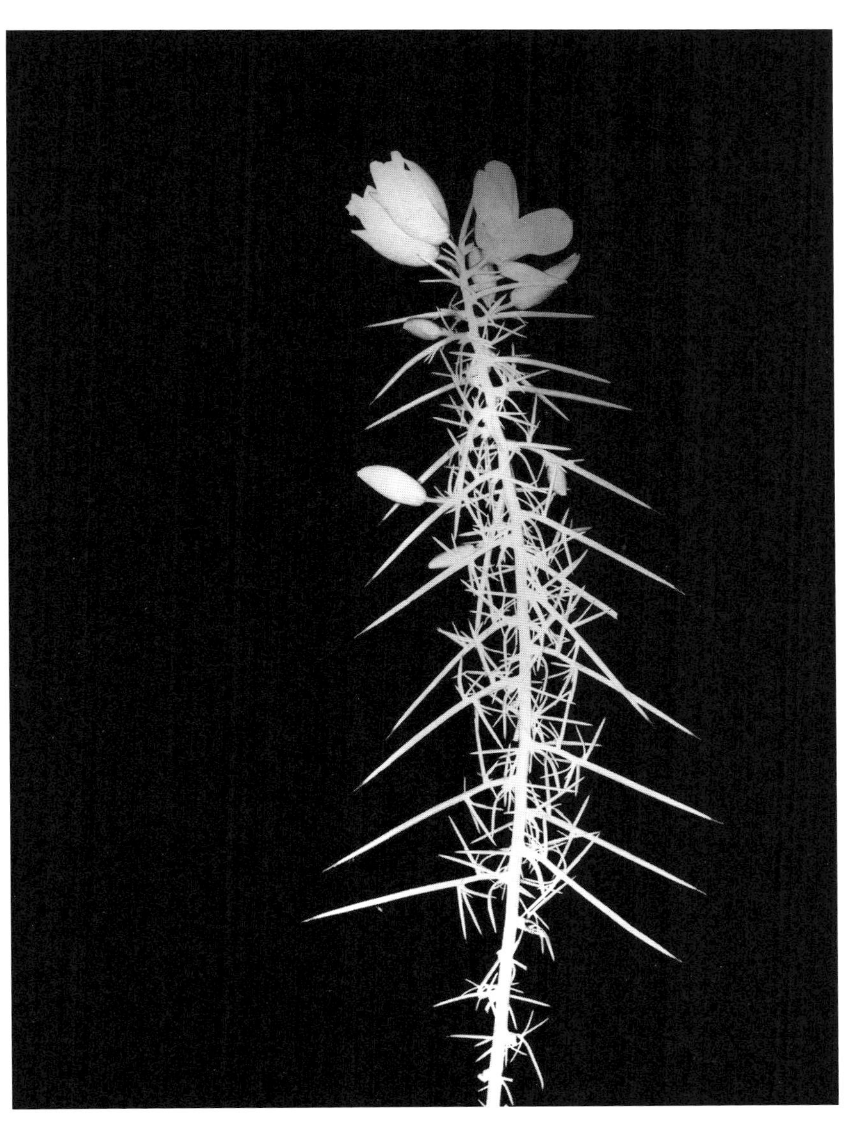

Gorse
Ulex europaeus

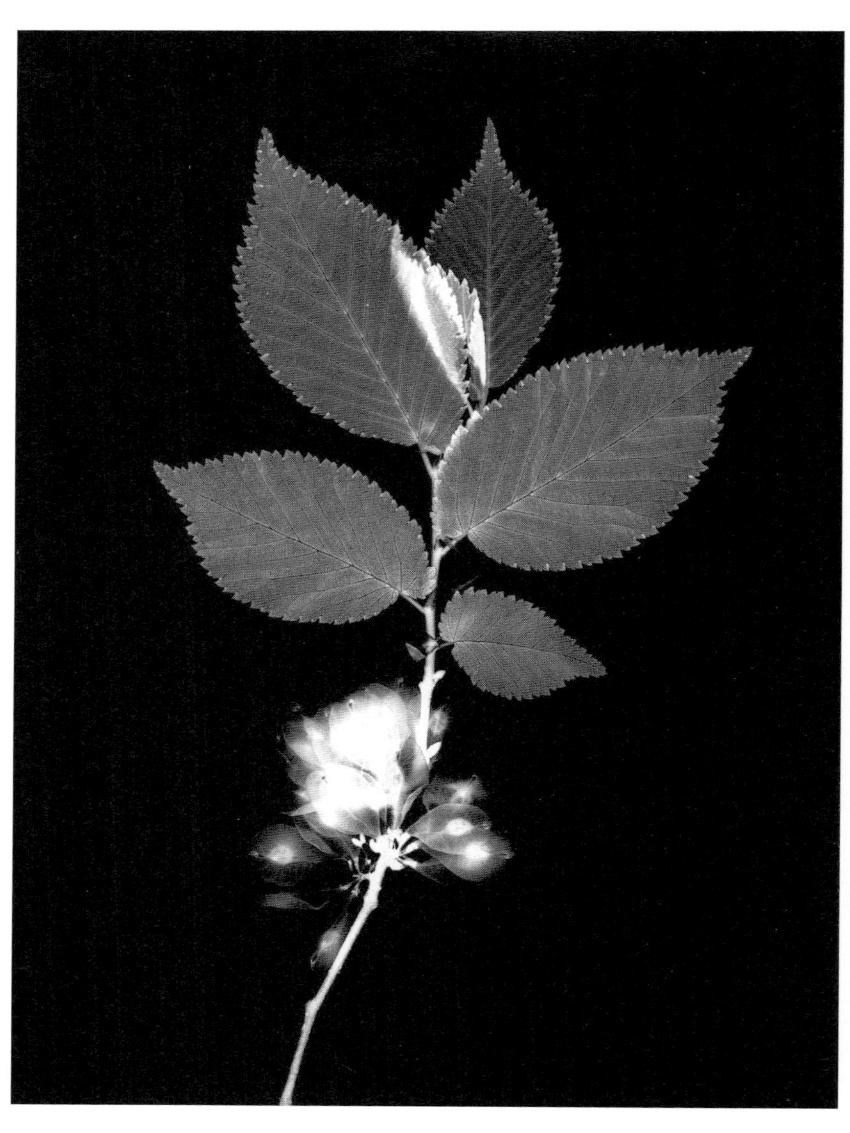

Wych Elm
Ulmus glabra

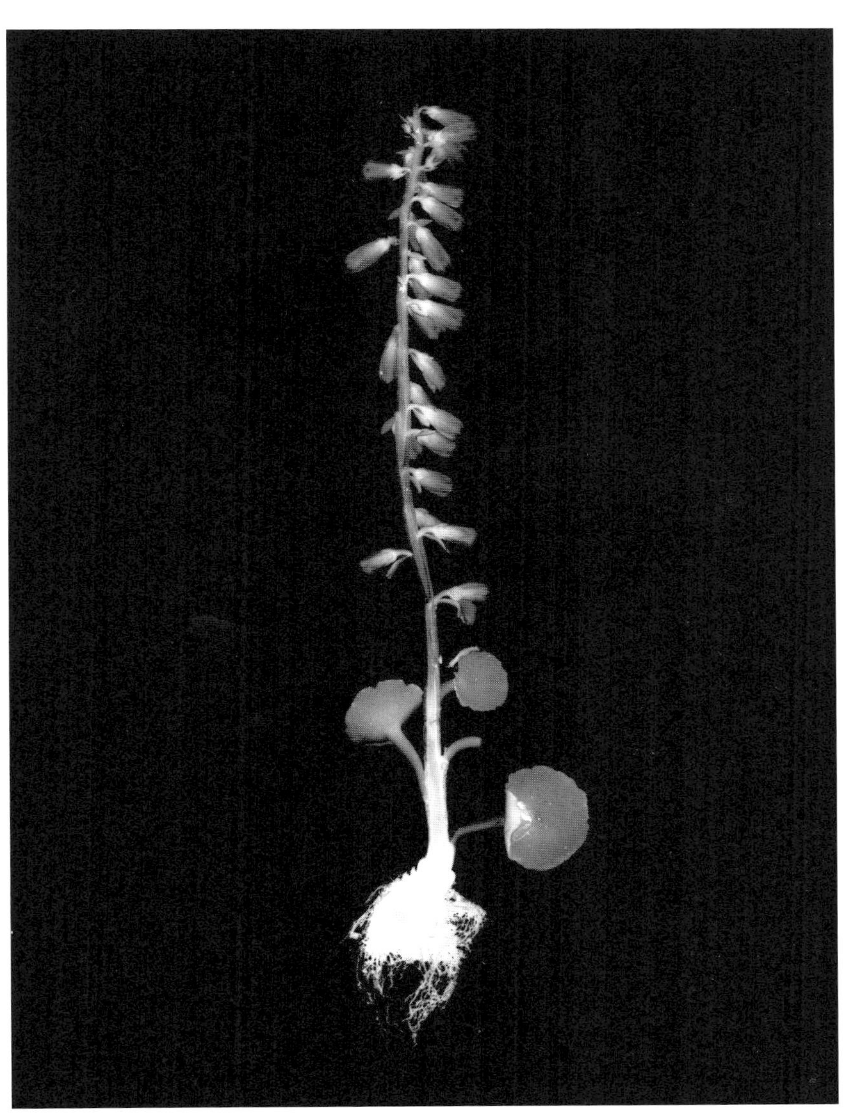

Navelwort
Umbilicus rupestris

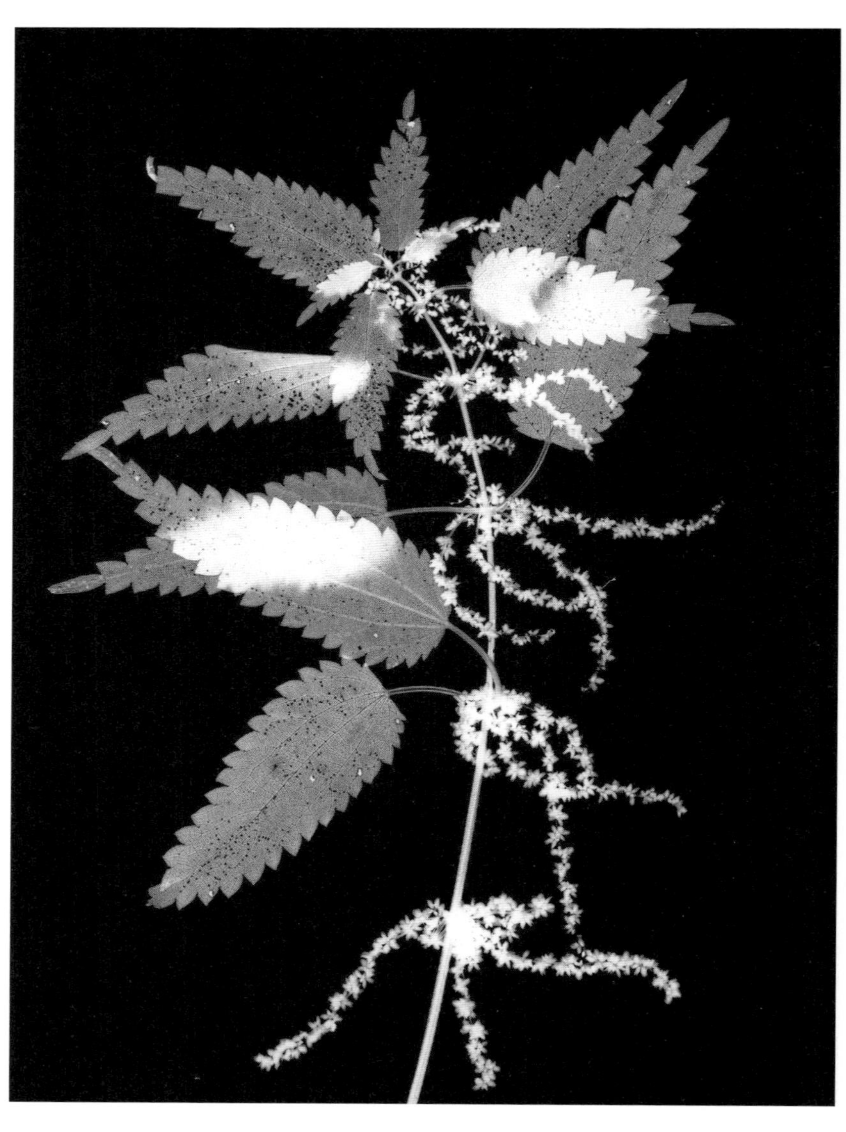

Stinging Nettle
Urtica dioica

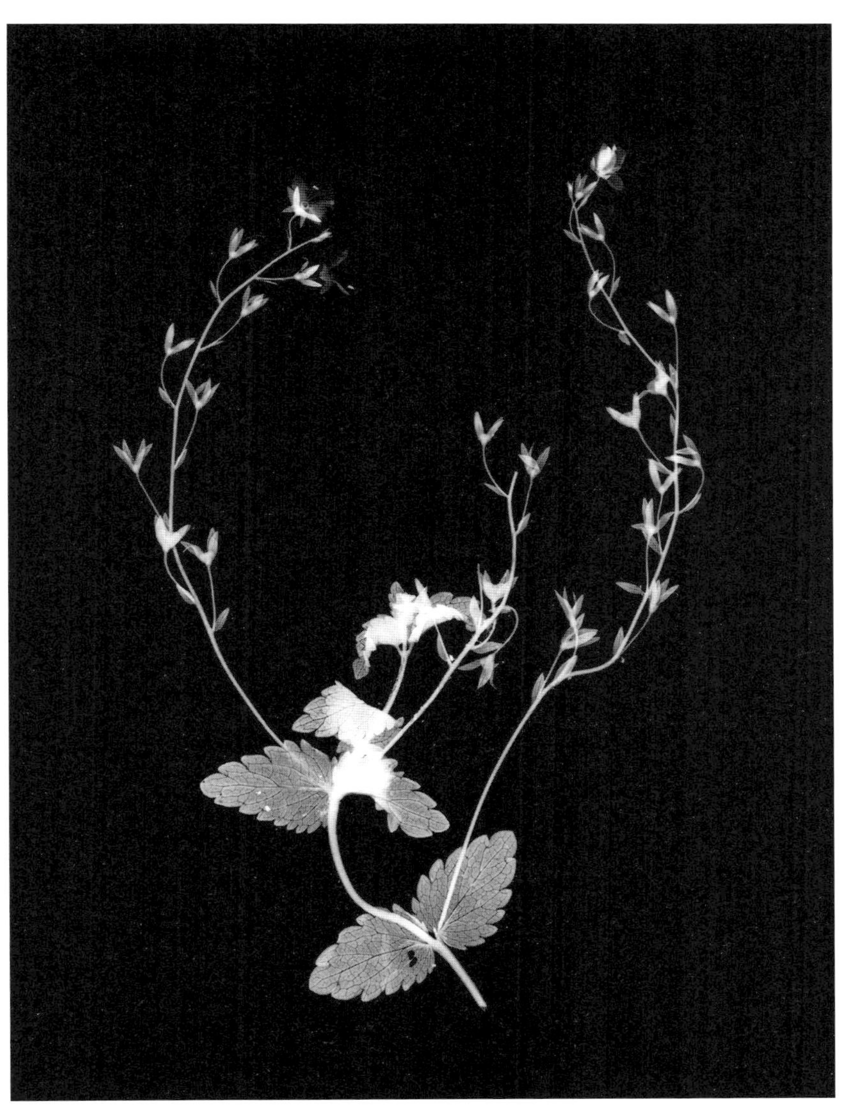

Common Field Speedwell
Veronica persica

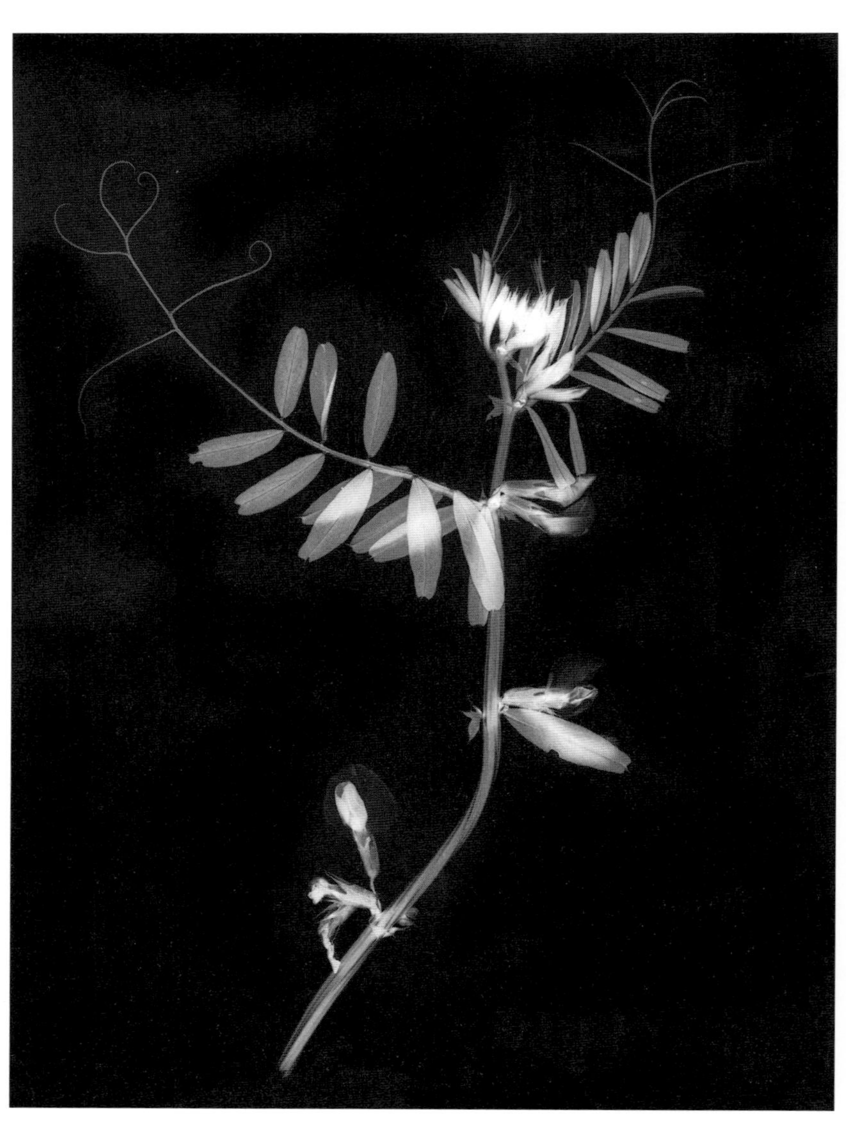

Common Vetch
Vicia sativa

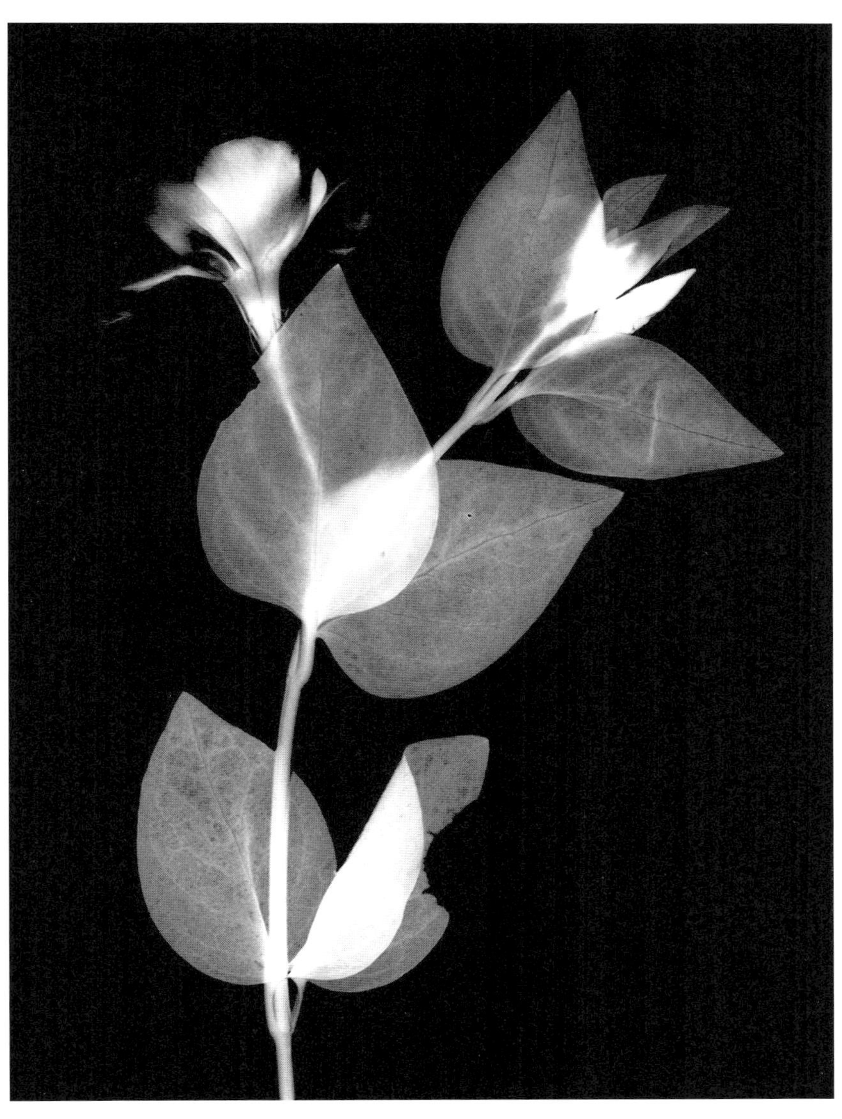

Lesser Periwinkle
Vinca minor

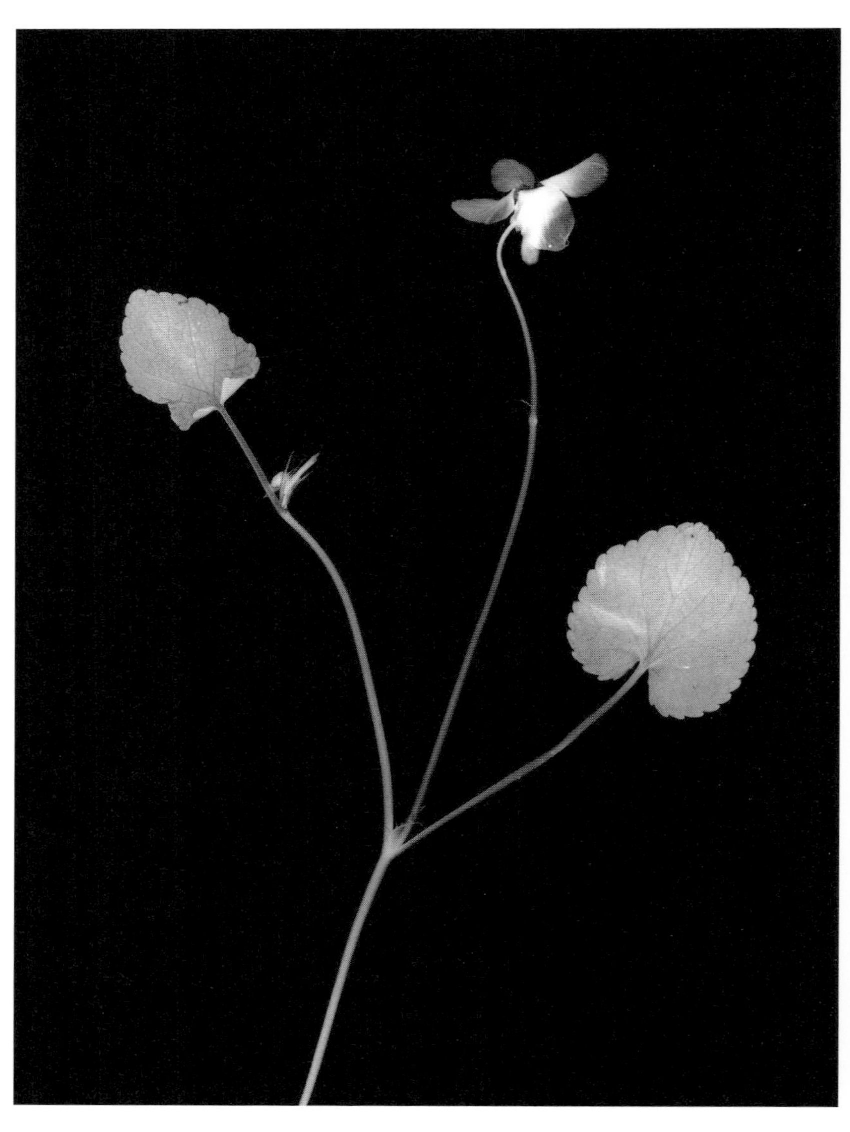

Dog Violet
Viola canina

Val Williams

Walking in the Margins

William Arnold's images of the common plants which flourish in the margins between the cultivated and the wild are hauntings—glimmers of life, the commonplace become miraculous: everyday Buddleia is a light cone making a luminous trajectory, humble Hedge Bedstraw redrawn as a map of an undiscovered galaxy. Photography has always been a kind of alchemy, transformation taking place in the time lapse between the making of the image and the realization of the material object. Arnold's photographs take the everyday, the weed gardens which flourish on every bit of abandoned ground and untended verge, always on the edges, largely overlooked, and transforms them into enchantments.

Photographers have been documenting plants since the beginning of the medium—during his early experiments in photography, inventor William Henry Fox Talbot made delicate calotypes of leaves, showing us how photography is able to fixate on the natural, drawing out and illuminating sculptural form. Botanist Anna Atkins made ethereal images of flowers and leaves in the mid-nineteenth century as she experimented with Herschel's cyanotype process, producing the remarkable *Photographs of British Algae: Cyanotype Impressions* between 1843 and 1853. The making of gardens and the growing of plants was necessarily documented photographically—the pioneering plantswoman Gertrude Jekyll, who worked as garden designer with architect Edwin Lutyens in the early years of the twentieth century, documented the many gardens she made and individual plants. The author of many books on plants and gardens, including *Wall and Water Gardens* (1901) and *Colour in the Flower Garden* (1908) Jekyll was an accomplished photographer, documenting many of the gardens she planted.

Professional gardener Charles Jones, who photographed the flowers, fruit and vegetables he grew during his tenure at Great

Ote Hall in Sussex and other country houses in the late nineteenth and early twentieth centuries, produced photographs of the cultivated natural world which are defined both by their objectivity and beauty. Like Arnold (who has paid homage to Jones in his 2018/19 series of lantern plates *Photographed after Charles Jones*), Jones avoided the picturesque and concentrated instead on the sharp sublimity of form and shape. Likewise, the pioneering colour photographer John Hinde, in his series of books on English flowers produced for Collins/Adprint, including *Annuals in Colour and Cultivation* (1949), made clear, sharply focussed photographs of garden flowers using techniques of colour photography learned in Germany before the outbreak of the Second World War. Photography formalised these horticultural hybrids, reiterating their move from nature.

Away from, or reacting against, the formality of gardening, natural history photographers of the '40s and '50s began to look at the wild margins of urban Britain. As editor of the *New Naturalist* series in the 1940s, photographer Eric Hosking realised that nature had to be made relevant to the city dweller, that the grand and picturesque could be replaced by the seemingly inconsequential plants and animals that were available to the suburban naturalist. *London's Natural History*, published in 1945 and edited by the naturalist R. S. R. Fitter, reestablished the natural in a country where much lay in ruins—in which the flora and fauna of the bomb site would become an invaluable resource for city naturalists, and which predicted the emergence of interest in marginal lands, both in photography and natural history writing. 157 species were discovered in England's bomb sites, "interlopers and opportunists, immigrants from southern Europe and north America. Their seeds had drifted in on returning soldiers' boots and transatlantic food aid, or had sprung to life after being buried for generations under concrete. The Canadian fleabane had reputedly arrived in Europe in the stuffing of a parrot sent to Germany."[1] Much as the pre- and post-war Shell Guides had made the English landscape desirable and attainable to motorists, and tourists, and W. G. Hoskins' *The Making of the English Landscape* (1955) presented the landscape not as a sublime mystery but a coherent system of signs, so *London's Natural History* made the wild city available to all.

For photographers and writers of the 1980s, '90s and onwards, the idea of the marginal became central. In Britain, the work of photographers such as Keith Arnatt, Raymond Moore and Jem Southam insisted that we take account of the unpicturesque— the landscape that is all around us—a neglected country pond, a utilitarian service station nestled in magnificent hills, a roadside verge. Writers and pyschogeographers including Iain Sinclair and Rachel Lichtenstein in their writings on marginal landscapes, (Sinclair in *London Orbital*, 2002, and Rachel Lichtenstein in *Estuary*, 2016) have conjured up the enchanted ordinary—what writer Blake Morrison has referred to as places of "subversive cultural energy".[2] Following in the footsteps of *London's Natural History*, and the emerging debate about ownership and steward-ship of nature, artists and writers began to explore marginal lands, with all the politics and social critiques which became an integral part of this interest in the unclaimed edgelands. Writer and environmentalist Marion Shoard, in her 1980 book *The Theft of the Countryside* and subsequent writings, drew attention to the fracturing of the landscape and its importance in our national consciousness. Many years later, in the 2011 publication *Edge-lands*, Paul Farley and Michael Symmons Roberts meditate on the untidy marginal landscapes that so often form an integral part of our memories: "For a long while, an entire childhood in fact, we wondered where the countryside actually was, or even if it really existed. Growing up on the edge of two cities—Liverpool and Manchester—in the early Seventies, it was easy enough to walk for a short while and soon find yourself lost in back lanes or waste ground, to follow the wooded perimeters of a golf course, an old path leading through scratchy shrubland, or the course of a drainage ditch."[3]

William Arnold's photographs, in *Suburban Herbarium*, refer-ence both this contemporary urge to map everyday wildness, with its bank of memories, as reflected in the work of Lichten-stein et al, and an older antiquarian inclination to collect, classify and define. The Royal Botanic Gardens at Kew defines herbaria, or a herbarium as "a collection of preserved plants stored, cata-logued, and arranged systematically for study by professionals and amateurs from many walks of life… a herbarium is a cross between a museum of priceless artefacts and a warehouse of birth certificates for plants; and acts as a source of information about plants—where they are found, what chemicals they have in them, when they flower, what they look like."[4]

Forensic botanist Professor Patricia Wiltshire writes about the garden as a repository of clues: "perhaps what you once thought of as small and compact has become something vast and unknown. Your garden, even the tiniest garden, holds so much more information than you can possibly assimilate. From the vantage point of a tiny pollen grain, even the smallest garden is a vast landscape of different terrains—all inter-connected as ecosystems are…".[5]

The photographs that make up Arnold's *Suburban Herbarium*, different as they are from the highly coloured botanical photographs we are accustomed to seeing in gardening books and plant catalogues, appear more as clues than as specimens—they are not the flowers and leaves that we would notice as we pass verges and hedges and the ragged edges of cultivation, but rather an idea of these plants, transmuted and transmitted through photographic methods which are magical and antiquarian. Arnold has applied the filter of art and technology, just as Wiltshire applies the filter of science, to make the world around us intelligible.

On receiving a gift of photographs from the inventor, Fox Talbot's sister-in-law called them "beautiful shadows". Having not yet perfected the technique of fixing the photographs, Fox Talbot's early images faded. One of those photographs is *Botanical Specimen 1* c.1835, in which the faint image of a periwinkle flower and its leaves glimmers on the paper's surface. It is preserved in the collection of the Gilman Paper Company in the United States and was included in a remarkable touring exhibition, *The Waking Dream*, in the early 1990s. To make the image, Fox Talbot laid the plant "directly on the top of a sheet of photosensitised paper, blocking the rays of the sun from darkening those portions it covered and thus leaving a light impression of its form…".[6] Fox Talbot was a serious and enthusiastic amateur botanist and he envisioned the accurate recording of such specimens to be among the most important practical applications of his invention. *Botanical Specimen 1* has almost disappeared, but its vitality and presence are undiminished.

Almost two hundred years after Fox Talbot made *Botanical Specimen 1*, William Arnold began to make images of the plants he discovered in the urban edgelands: writing about his work, Arnold described how the images in *Suburban Herbarium* were made during the course of a regular lunchtime walk—a break from a teaching post in a "small but expanding city". He cites botanists James Wandersee and Elizabeth Schussler, writing in *Plant Science Bulletin* and their theory of 'Plant Blindness'—"the inability to see or notice the plants in one's own environment"[7] as part of the impetus for the photographic series he produced. For Arnold, the daily walk was an assertion of independence in the face of a rigid nine to five working day, the work that he made "an edgelands homage to Victorian botany". In this short essay, he talks about "outskirt landscapes of disappointment… the building sites, road verge, business parks, wasteland and identikit housing, where were it not for the necessity of stable employment nearby, one would never choose to spend time".[8]

The 'rediscovery' of nineteenth century photography methods and a re-adoption of the analogue in the face of digital perfection, is a central part of Arnold's process. The careful collection and transport of 'specimens' to the darkroom, where they are "projected, enlarged and logged as pure form—study in silver-gelatin" is reminiscent not only of photography pioneers, but also of the eighteenth-century explorer-plant collector. The colonial ambition to acquire and commercialise plant specimens from far away countries, together with an aristocratic desire in Britain for exotic and hard to find species to plant on expanding and often re-modelled estates, resulted in an almost frenetic phase of collection. Many, including Francis Masson, who sailed with Captain Cook to South Africa and subsequently made many more collecting expeditions, were sent by the Royal Botanic Gardens at Kew, and China was a particularly rewarding territory for plant hunters. On his website, Arnold quotes explorer Mungo Park, who, even during his greatest vicissitudes in Africa, was able to marvel at the beauty of a moss. Early plant collectors were intrepid and often in danger—broken legs, malaria, and death by trapping were the fates of the discoverers of those great suburban garden plants the lupin, the rhododendron and the camellia. William Arnold avoids these exotics and looks instead at native weeds—though even he is tempted by garden invaders—"there isn't any Japanese Knotweed on my walk but there is some Himalayan Honeysuckle—it's beautiful but non-native and invasive".[9]

Suburban Herbarium is a homage to and a critique of plant collecting. While hybrids of the original collected plants are now a staple of our northern European gardens, plants were as much of a colonial commodity as spices or textiles, gemstones, metals or works of art. The curators of the *Radical Botany* exhibition at the Eden Project remark that: "Plants have been traded, sold and moved across the globe, their travels mimicking the migration of people through time. Unfortunately, with this movement, and the colonising of land, whole ecosystems have often been disrupted and species lost."[10] But if *Suburban Herbarium* can be seen as part of an ecological critique, it is also a celebration—of walking, of finding, of the possibilities of photography, of the plants themselves, fragile and disregarded, here made into sublime objects of beauty. Arnold makes no claim to be a 'walking artist' in the mode of Hamish Fulton or Richard Long—he walks not to explore, as Fulton does, or to construct, in the manner of Long; for him, walking is a kind of refuge, a meditative period of collecting and recording. These photograms surprise and delight, they glimmer like spectres—*Medicago lupulina*, spiky tendrils illuminated, *Lycesteria formosa*, a sudden fiery blotch, the harlequinade of *Eschscholzia californica*; the mystery of language combined with the magic of photography, the ordinary made stupendous.

1. Richard Mabey, 'News of birds and blossoming', *The Guardian*, 13 March 2009.
2. Blake Morrison, review of *Estuary*, the *Guardian*, 20 October 2016.
3. Paul Farley and Michael Symmons Roberts, *Edgelands*, London, 2011.
4. 'What is a Herbarium?' kew.org
5. Patricia Wiltshire, *Traces: The memoir of a forensic scientist and criminal investigator*, London, 2019.
6. Maria Morris Hambourg, *The Waking Dream: Photography's First Century*, New York, 1993.
7. James H. Wandersee and Elisabeth E. Schussler, 'Toward a Theory of Plant Blindness' *Plant Science Bulletin*, Vol.47, No.1, Columbus, 2001.
8. williamarnold.net/Suburban-Herbarium
9. 'Suburban Herbarium', interview with Diva Harris, 27 June 2016, caughtbytheriver.net
10. 'Radical Botany', edenproject.com

Val Williams is a writer and curator and UAL Professor of the History and Culture of Photography at the London College of Communication. She is an editor of the *Journal of Photography and Culture*. Exhibition projects, curated and co-curated, include How We Are (Tate Britain), Seaside Photographed (Turner Contemporary and touring); Martin Parr Retrospective (Barbican Art Gallery); Warworks (V&A); Tish Murtha (Photographers Gallery). Authored and co-authored books include: *Daniel Meadows: Edited Photographs* (Photoworks); *Ken. To be Destroyed: Sara Davidmann* (ed.) (Schilt); *Seaside Photographed* (Thames and Hudson); *Portraits in a Chinese Studio: Grace Lau* (ed.) (Parakeet Books). She is a member of the Board of Fast Forward: Women in Photography and co-convenor of the Fast Forward conferences at Tate Modern and National Gallery of Art, Vilnius, Lithuania.

Index of Plants

Polypody, Common 81
Polystichum setiferum 82
Poppy, California 47
——, Flanders 79
Potentilla reptans 83
—— *sterilis* 84
Primrose 85
Primula vulgaris 85
Prunella vulgaris 86
Prunus avium 87
—— *spinosa* 88
Pteridium aquilinum 89

Ragged Robin 72
Ragwort 67
Ranunculus repens 90
Rapeseed 25
Rosa canina 91
Rose, Dog 91
Rubus fructicosus 92
Rumex obtusifolius 93

Salix cinerea 94
Sedge, Pendulous 29
Self-heal 86
Silene dioica 95
Sloe 88
Solanum dulcamara 96
Sonchus oleraceus 97
Sorrel, Yellow Wood 78
Sowthistle, Common 97
Speedwell, Common Field 109
——, Shining 55
St John's Wort, Slender 66
Stachys sylvatica 98
Stellaria holostea 99
Stitchwort, Greater 99
Strawberry, Barren 84
Sumbuscus nigra 100
Sycamore 13
Symphytum officinale 101
—— *tuberosum* 102

Taraxacum officinale 103
Thistle, Creeping 33
Toadflax, Ivy-leaved 41
Trifolium pratense 104
Turnip, Wild 24

Ulex europaeus 105
Ulmus glabra 106
Umbilicus rupestris 107
Urtica dioica 108

Veronica persica 109
Vetch, Common 110
——, Kidney 20
Vicia sativa 110
Vinca minor 111
Viola canina 112
Violet, Dog 112

Willow, Grey 94
Willowherb, Great 45
——, Hoary 44
Woundwort, Hedge 98

Yarrow 14